"BETTER DEAD THAN RED!"

A NOSTALGIC LOOK AT THE GOLDEN YEARS OF RUSSIAPHOBIA, RED-BAITING, AND OTHER COMMIE MADNESS

HYPERION

NEW YORK

MICHAEL BARSON

For copyright acknowledgments, see page 143.

Text Copyright © 1992 Michael Barson

Design by Victor Weaver

First Edition
10 9 8 7 6 5 4 3 2 1

DEDICATION

To Bill Weete, who liked the idea. We miss you, big guy.

ACKNOWLEDGMENTS

My heartfelt thanks to the following folks, who contributed above and beyond the call:
to Victor Weaver, deity of design
to John Kisch, for pics without peer
to Leslie Wells, for editing exquisite
to Ed Cohen, for refinements royale
to Henry Fera, Ron and Howard Mandlebaum, and Eric Rachlis, for photos phantastique
to John Benson, Bill Emerson, and Art Spiegelman, for materials most marvelous
to Anne Scatto, for suggestions sublime
to Leslie Herzik, for inputting into infinity
to Nancy Stauffer, for support so staunch
And of course to Jeannie, for all of the above and then some

WHAT IF THEY GAVE A COLD WAR AND NOBODY CAME?

The price of caviar may drop!

That bit of news, reported in *The Wall Street Journal* as this volume goes to press, seems to be the tidiest symbol of all that has transpired lately with the dissolution of the Union of Soviet Socialist Republics. No more hammer and sickle . . . no more Gossport, the Soviet Olympic agency. Things have been so bad over there that Peter Jennings--merely the top electronic journalist in America-- actually believed *Forbes*' planted story about the Russians having to auction the preserved corpse of V. I. Lenin to raise $15 million for expenses. How the mighty have fallen, indeed.

Of course, the roots of the Soviet Empire's demise can be traced back several decades, long before the world had ever heard the words *perestroika* and *glasnost*. Warning bells should have rung in the mid-sixties when Soviet UN attachés filed reports after seeing Liza Minnelli in *Flora, the Red Menace* on Broadway, and the comedy *The Russians Are Coming, the Russians Are Coming* in movie theaters. Certainly the sight of Rocky and Bullwinkle besting the hapless Commie spies Boris and Natasha in the cartoon series *Rocky and His Friends* way back in 1959 --before the Berlin Wall was built, for gosh sakes!--should have tipped them off. Let's face it: if the Russkies were still as frightening after Khrushchev as they had appeared to us in the forties and fifties, James Bond wouldn't have had to match wits with imaginary organizations like SMERSH and SPECTRE to save the world.

What's happened is anticlimactic, and more than a little bit sad. Imagine us sending aid to the Evil Empire! (Even if it will soon be known as "the Benign Commonwealth.") Joe McCarthy must be spinning in his grave. And what would Arthur "Guitar Boogie" Smith, who penned the ditty "Mr. Stalin, You're Eatin' Too High on the Hog," back in 1950, think?

All those millions, billions, and trillions of dollars we spent trying to contain the voracious Soviet Bear . . . all the federal agencies dedicated to the proposition that, at any minute, America would be seized by the thousands of highly trained Red operatives lurking in the corridors of the State Department . . . all those dumb bomb drills and high-octane science courses America's schoolchildren had to suffer through to catch up with the brainier Russians . . . all the weekends spent stocking the bomb shelter with the best in canned goods and paperback novels . . . all those nights when we couldn't sleep for worrying about whether *our* ICBMs were quicker on the draw than *their* ICBMs . . . all of this, and so much more, and for what? Was it merely to maintain the price of caviar? To give us someone to root against in the Olympics? (How *about* that shafting our basketball team got in '72? You can't tell *me* those refs weren't working for the KGB!) The Cold War couldn't have been engineered just to give the boys in the Pentagon something to spend their money on, could it?

"Better Dead Than Red!" was a cry once proudly shared from sea to shining sea among all right-minded Americans (whose pockets and pocketbooks always seemed to bulge with copies of *Reader's Digest*, for some reason). It therefore seemed an appropriate title for this collection of residue from the Cold War--the flotsam and jetsam that delineates just how far gone America once was. All of the material you'll find within these pages is "real"--at least, as real as the Cold War itself was. For today it seems as though a mist has settled over the American Memory; call it selective amnesia. For most of us, only a few highlights remain: J. Edgar Hoover? A creep, to be sure. Joe McCarthy? A bully. Alger Hiss--wasn't he some kind of spy? And then it starts to get fuzzy.

But the Cold War wasn't just something played out by the pros in Moscow and Washington-- although they did more than their share. *All* of us contributed to keeping that state of mind alive-- even this writer, who at the age of seven rushed home to show off his newly mastered "civil defense crouch." It was no shared hallucination; the fact is, for twenty years or so, America lost its collective mind. Yes, the Cold War really did happen, even on Main Street, U.S.A. And *"BETTER DEAD THAN RED!"* is going to take you back there.

—Michael Barson

COMMUNIST PARTY INDUCTION PLEDGE
(CIRCA 1942)

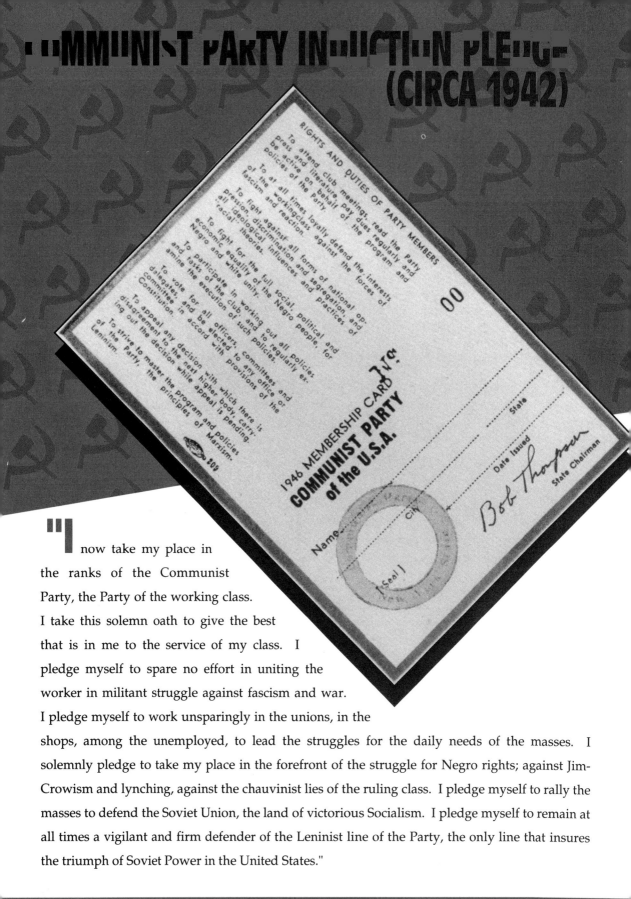

RIGHTS AND DUTIES OF PARTY MEMBERS

To attend club meetings, read the Party press and literature, pay dues regularly and be active on behalf of the program and policies of the Party.

To at all times loyally defend the interests of the workingclass against the forces of fascism and reaction.

To fight against all forms of national oppression, discrimination and segregation, and all ideological influences and practices of racial theories.

To fight for the full social, political and economic equality of the Negro people, for Negro and white unity.

To participate in working out all policies and to regularly examine the execution of such policies.

To vote for all officers, committees and delegates, and be elected to any office or Committee, in accord with provisions of the Constitution.

To appeal any decision with which there is disagreement to the next higher body, carrying out the decision while appeal is pending.

To strive to master the program and policies of the Party, the principles of Marxism-Leninism.

1946 MEMBERSHIP CARD
COMMUNIST PARTY
of the U.S.A.

Name

Date Issued

State

Bob Thompson
State Chairman

"I now take my place in the ranks of the Communist Party, the Party of the working class. I take this solemn oath to give the best that is in me to the service of my class. I pledge myself to spare no effort in uniting the worker in militant struggle against fascism and war. I pledge myself to work unsparingly in the unions, in the shops, among the unemployed, to lead the struggles for the daily needs of the masses. I solemnly pledge to take my place in the forefront of the struggle for Negro rights; against Jim-Crowism and lynching, against the chauvinist lies of the ruling class. I pledge myself to rally the masses to defend the Soviet Union, the land of victorious Socialism. I pledge myself to remain at all times a vigilant and firm defender of the Leninist line of the Party, the only line that insures the triumph of Soviet Power in the United States."

The Ukrainian delegation at the physical culture parade in Moscow.

THE FIRST RED SCARE

The Russian Revolution of November 1917 excited members of the American Left, if Warren Beatty's film *Reds* is at all accurate. For most Americans, though, that historic moment was of far less import than, say, World War I, which we were then in the thick of. But one night in June of 1919, the newly appointed U.S. attorney general, A. Mitchell Palmer, had his sleep interrupted by the sound of a bomb exploding on his front doorstep. Across the street, FDR, then assistant secretary of the navy, heard the blast and rushed to the Palmers' aid--stepping over pieces of the unfortunate bomber, who apparently had tripped and blown himself up, thus becoming the sole casualty of the evening. After it emerged that bombs had exploded on the doorsteps of high-ranking lawmakers in eight other cities that same night, the first Red scare began to sweep the country. The next day's *New York Times* reported that the attack was "plainly of Bolshevik or IWW origin."

As Curt Gentry reports in his splendid *J. Edgar Hoover: The Man and the Secrets* (Norton, 1991), Palmer—"the Fighting Quaker"—wanted to create special task forces to investigate and prosecute the anarchists who were now holding America in the grip of terror (when they weren't busy blowing themselves to smithereens). He begged Congress to increase funding for the Department of Justice to meet this sudden crisis, but was turned down. Undaunted, Palmer and his chief assistant, Francis Garvan, went before the Senate and convinced that body that the wave of bombings was part of a well-organized conspiracy to overthrow the U.S. government, and that a mass revolution was being readied for the Fourth of July. Alarmed, the Senate promptly gave Palmer the extra $500,000 he wanted.

Now properly funded, Palmer and his lieutenants decided that the best method of squelching the new menace was to implement a mass roundup of "alien radicals"--leaving non-alien American anarchists free to wreak havoc, presumably--who could then be deported in short order. (Of course, the Immigration Department was the only agency authorized to deport undesirables, and there was no actual law on the books that prohibited membership in the IWW, the Communist Party, or even Anarchists Anonymous-- but, what the heck, this was an emergency.) The $500,000 appropriation was put to work establishing a new agency within Justice, the function of which would be to gather information about radicals from local police, the military, the Bureau of Investigation, and John Q. Citizen. To head the new Anti-Radical Division, as it was first called, Garvan selected an up-and-comer from Justice who had a little experience working with the Enemy Alien Registration boys. He was only twenty-four years old, but there was something magical about him. His name was John Edgar Hoover.

A former librarian, Hoover immediately began collating membership lists of subversive organizations, like the IWW, with names supplied by local Red squads and private detective agencies. In a flash he had over 150,000 names to work with, including the thirty-odd thousand membership of the two branches of the American Communist movement, the Communist Labor Party and the Communist Party of America, bitter rivals who had split apart after an intramural dispute at the Socialist Party convention in Chicago in 1919. Studying the works of Marx and Lenin to better know the mind of his enemy, Hoover soon came to the conclusion that Communism was "the most evil, monstrous conspiracy against man since time began." (What about *before* time began?)

  With the agency renamed the General Intelligence Division (GID), Palmer and Hoover worked hand-in-hand to coordinate a raid on a national scale of the Federation of the Union of Russian Workers, an organization comprised of Russian immigrants who probably wouldn't have recognized a bomb if it was sitting on a table in the middle of their Annual Picnic. On the second anniversary of the Russian Revolution (November 7, 1919), agents of the GID and the Bureau of Investigation, along with local police promptly at 8:00 P.M. swooped down on the Russian People's Houses in twelve cities. This test raid, which netted 184 hapless club members, worked smoothly and got the fledgling GID lots of swell publicity, especially when the "blasphemous creatures" (*New York Times*) were deported to Russia on a ramshackle ship named the *Buford*. Joining the bewildered and bruised Federation of the Union of Russian Workers on the voyage were a handful of genuine anarchists, the most notorious of them being Emma Goldman--the "Red Queen of Anarchy," as the press christened her--who supposedly had planned the assassination of President McKinley back in 1901. (Her speeches and pamphlets in favor of free love probably were even more noxious to the GID than her radical politics.)

  In the flush of success, Hoover and Palmer moved ahead with their plans for a second, more comprehensive series of raids. Three thousand warrants of arrest were prepared for the mass roundup of alien radicals in thirty-three cities. On the night of January 2, 1920, some ten thousand suspects were arrested around the country--many without the benefit of a warrant, nor with advice of their right to counsel. Six thousand of them were released within a few days, once it was determined they weren't Party members. The unlucky four thousand who remained soon learned they were being held for deportation to Russia in a series of "Soviet Arks."

But what at first appeared to be a triumph for Palmer and Hoover soon turned to ashes in their mouths, as details of the illegal arrests became known to outraged lawmakers across the U.S. The outcry was so loud that, on June 1, Attorney General A. Mitchell Palmer was hauled before the House Rules Committee to defend the actions of the GID and the Department of Justice in the Red raids. With Hoover at his side, Palmer described the arrestees as "moral rats" whose "sly and crafty eyes" revealed "cruelty, insanity, and crime," and whose "lopsided faces, sloping brows and misshapen features" clearly indicated congenital thuggery of the Communist persuasion. He went on to deny that anyone's rights had been abrogated, or that force or violence had been used during or after the arrests. (That must have come as news to the hundreds of aliens whose heads had been used for batting practice by the enthusiastic constables, as depicted in *The New York Times*.)

Palmer escaped formal chastisement by the Rules Committee, though it is doubtful they believed a word of the 209-page statement he read into the record. But "the Great Red Hunter," who longed for the Democratic Party's nomination for the Presidency, was further humiliated by having to again defend himself early in 1921, this time before the Senate Judiciary Committee. His political hopes now dashed, Palmer began updating his résumé in November, when the Republican Warren G. Harding was elected President.

But while the first Red Scare was now over, a pattern had been set that would be repeated many times in the years to come. J. Edgar Hoover, who would assume the directorship of the Bureau of Investigation in 1924 (the same year Stalin rose to power in Russia . . . fancy that!) would spend the rest of his terrible and terribly long career bashing Reds at every opportunity, be they veterans of the Spanish Civil War, well-meaning fellow travelers, "moral rats," Supreme Court justices, or just big-mouthed liberals. (Even lefty Pablo Picasso was deemed worthy of his own FBI file, in the event he ever decided to visit these shores.) For fifty years, the imminent danger of a Communist takeover was always foremost in Hoover's beady little mind. It must have been a supreme disappointment to him that no one ever made much of an effort to bring it to pass.

"FORMERLY RED SALUTE"

HARRY M. GOETZ
presents

Barbara STANWYCK
RED SALUTE

with
ROBERT YOUNG

HARDIE ALBRIGHT · RUTH DONNELLY · CLIFF EDWARDS
GORDON JONES · PAUL STANTON

The EDWARD SMALL production

a RELIANCE picture · Directed by SIDNEY LANFIELD
Released thru UNITED ARTISTS

Photofest

Archive Photos

After that classic romantic comedy *It Happened One Night* swept the Academy Awards for 1934, a rash of imitators appeared in 1935. One of the quirkier knock-offs was *Red Salute*, which subverted the usual conventions of the genre by making one of its principal characters a Communist student radical.

When a rich girl, played by Barbara Stanwyck, is caught hanging around with a campus agitator (Hardie Albright), her father yanks her out of college and sends her south of the border to cool off. There she meets--and, naturally, falls for--a handsome Border Patrolman (Robert Young), whose straight-arrow ways quickly reform her leftist proclivities. The usual 674 plot complications follow, leading to the film's big wind-up: Albright and his Red buddies are soundly thrashed by Young and the rosy-cheeked student body. A pleasant diversion, *Red Salute* did not sweep the Academy Awards for 1935.

COMMUNIST ACTIVITIES UNCOVERED IN AMERICAN COLLEGES!

FROM TODAY'S HEADLINES...

Comes a startling story of the RED MENACE at work in our schools...planting seeds of treason among the men and women of tomorrow!

EDWARD SMALL *Presents*

Barbara **STANWYCK**
Robert **YOUNG**

in

RUNAWAY DAUGHTER

formerly "RED SALUTE"

TRUE! TIMELY! TERRIFIC!

with HARDIE ALBRIGHT · CLIFF EDWARDS
RUTH DONNELLY · GORDON JONES
PAUL STANTON

RE RELEASED BY SCREEN GUILD PRODUCTIONS

Eighteen years later, the film was given a second life when some enterprising accountant decided that the feverish headlines of the day (ROSENBERGS EXECUTED AS ATOM SPIES! . . . . MALENKOV CLAIMS THE HYDROGEN BOMB!) had created a demand for movies with anti-Communist messages. A new marketing campaign was devised--"A startling story of the RED MENACE at work in our schools . . . planting the seed of treason among the men and women of tomorrow!"--and the film was given a new title, *Runaway Daughter*. But audiences easily recognized it for the recycled 1935 product that it was. After all, in 1953, campus radicals wouldn't have been punched out as punishment; they would have been jailed or deported.

A deluxe magazine published by the State Art Publishing House in Moscow during the height of the purge trials, *U.S.S.R. in Construction* was produced in five different languages: Russian, English, French, Spanish, and German. Bannered with that familiar slogan, "Proletarians of all countries, unite!" the lively issue for November-December 1938 cost a mere twenty-five cents in the U.S., and was also available by subscription. (I wonder if Hoover was on their mailing list?) The attractive flower motif was designed by "collective farm woman Tatiana Chetyerik," the credits tells us, while the full-color, tipped-in plate of Stalin you see reproduced here so humbly is from a tapestry woven by a group of collective-farm women in Kiev's Folk Art Workshops. All in all, an incredible bargain for a quarter, and if Stalin hadn't blown it by aligning himself with Hitler a few months later, *U.S.S.R. in Construction* could have been bigger than *Life*, *Look*, and *Reader's Digest* combined.

U.S.S.R. IN CONSTRUCTION • № 11–12 • 1938

THE SOUTHERN PART OF OUR COUNTRY, WITH ITS RICH STORES OF GRAIN, COAL AND IRON, HAS ALWAYS ATTRACTED THE GREEDY GAZE OF FOREIGN PLUNDERERS. IN EARLIER TIMES THE UKRAINE WAS SUBJECT TO THE FREQUENT RAIDS OF POLOVTZI, TATARS, LITHUANIANS AND POLES. IN THE ERA OF CAPITALISM, AS STALIN SAID, "...THE UKRAINE WAS EXPLOITED BY THE IMPERIALISTS OF THE WEST SURREPTITIOUSLY, SO TO SPEAK, WITHOUT 'MILITARY OPERATIONS.' BY STARTING BIG INDUSTRIES (COAL, METAL, ETC.) IN THE UKRAINE AND GRABBING THE MAJORITY OF THEIR SHARES, THE IMPERIALISTS OF FRANCE, BELGIUM AND ENGLAND SUCKED THE BLOOD OF THE UKRAINIAN PEOPLE 'LEGALLY,' WITHOUT NOISE AND FUSS."

THE GREAT OCTOBER SOCIALIST REVOLUTION, ACCOMPLISHED UNDER THE LEADERSHIP OF THE PARTY OF LENIN AND STALIN, TURNED OVER THE LAND AND INDUSTRIES OF THE UKRAINE TO THE UKRAINIAN PEOPLE. BUT THE IMPERIALISTS OF THE WEST FOUND IT HARD TO RECONCILE THEMSELVES TO THE FACT AND ENDEAVOURED, IN CONJUNCTION WITH THE COUNTER-REVOLUTIONARIES OF RUSSIA AND THE UKRAINE, TO ENSLAVE THE UKRAINIAN PEOPLE. BUT THEY FAILED TO FASTEN THE YOKE ON THIS SOVIET PEOPLE, WHO STARTED A WAR FOR THE LIBERATION OF THEIR COUNTRY. IN THEIR HEROIC STRUGGLE THE UKRAINIAN PEOPLE WERE HELPED BY STALIN'S BRILLIANT STRATEGIC PLANS AND WERE WHOLEHEARTEDLY SUPPORTED BY THE RUSSIAN PEOPLE. AND THE ALLIANCE OF SOVIET NATIONS DEFEATED THE ALLIANCE OF HOME AND FOREIGN REACTIONARIES.

NOW THE UKRAINE IS LIVING A FULL-BLOODED AND CREATIVE LIFE AS ONE OF THE RICHEST REPUBLICS OF THE SOVIET UNION. THE BINS OF ITS COLLECTIVE FARMS ARE BURSTING WITH GOLDEN GRAIN. ITS FIELDS ARE CULTIVATED BY TENS OF THOUSANDS OF TRACTORS, HARVESTER COMBINES AND OTHER COMPLEX MACHINES OPERATED BY THE YOUNG SKILLED MECHANICS OF SOCIALIST AGRICULTURE. THE STAKHANOVITES AND SHOCK-WORKERS OF THE DONBAS, ARMED WITH UP-TO-DATE EQUIPMENT, THE NEW AND RECONSTRUCTED METAL PLANTS OF THE LEFT BANK OF THE DNIEPER, THE IRON MINES OF KRIVOY ROG, THE SUGAR REFINERIES OF THE RIGHT BANK SUPPLY THE SOCIALIST COUNTRY WITH ABUNDANT COAL, METAL, ORE AND SUGAR.

HUNDREDS OF NEW MILLS AND FACTORIES HAVE BEEN ERECTED IN THE UKRAINE DURING THE PERIOD OF THE STALIN FIVE-YEAR PLANS.

THE DREAM OF THE GREAT UKRAINIAN POET, TARAS SHEVCHENKO, OF A FREE AND HAPPY UKRAINE HAS COME TRUE. HER PEOPLE ARE MAKING SPLENDID CONTRIBUTIONS TO SOCIALIST LITERATURE, MUSIC AND ART.

THE TROTSKYITE, BUKHARINITE AND BOURGEOIS NATIONALIST AGENTS OF FASCIST ESPIONAGE SERVICES, DREAMED OF LAYING THE YOKE OF CAPITALIST SLAVERY ON THIS FREE PEOPLE AND DRENCHING THE SOVIET SOIL IN BLOOD. IN THEIR RAGE, THEY TRIED TO CHECK THE VICTORIOUS MARCH OF SOCIALISM AND TURN BACK THE WHEEL OF HISTORY. BUT THEY MISCALCULATED.

THEY WERE DEFEATED AND SMASHED BY THE FIRM HAND OF THE UKRAINIAN PEOPLE, LED BY THE PARTY OF LENIN AND STALIN.

KIEV, THE CAPITAL OF THE UKRAINE, REFLECTS THE FLOURISHING PROGRESS OF THE COUNTRY. KIEV HAS PLAYED AN INTIMATE PART IN THE HISTORY OF THE UKRAINIAN AND RUSSIAN PEOPLES. IT IS "THE MOTHER OF RUSSIAN CITIES," A CENTRE OF EARLY RUSSIAN CULTURE. EVERY CORNER OF THE CITY BREATHES THE MEMORY OF REMOTE HISTORICAL EVENTS.

KIEV RANKS AMONG THE MOST BEAUTIFUL CITIES OF EUROPE. IT SUFFERED SEVERELY DURING THE INVASIONS OF THE GERMANS AND THE POLES AND UNDER THE RULE OF THE BANDIT WHITEGUARDS. BY THE END OF THE CIVIL WAR THE ECONOMIC LIFE OF THE CITY HAD BEEN SHATTERED; MANY OF ITS HOUSES AND BUILDINGS HAD BEEN DESTROYED BY FIRE AND SHELL; THE BEAUTIFUL TSEPNOI BRIDGE HAD BEEN BLOWN UP BY THE RETREATING POLES....

GREAT IS OUR ADMIRATION OF THE CAPITAL OF SOVIET UKRAINE TODAY, WITH ITS BEAUTIFUL MAIN STREETS, MAGNIFICENT NEW BUILDINGS, RECONSTRUCTED AND WELL-PAVED SUBURBS, GRANITE-LINED EMBANKMENTS ALONG THE DNIEPER, STADIUMS, SCHOOLS—ALL WITNESSING TO THE PERSISTENT AND DEVOTED EFFORTS OF THE PARTY AND NON-PARTY BOLSHEVIKS OF THE UKRAINE.

IN TSARIST TIMES, KIEV WAS MAINLY A COMMERCIAL CITY. IN 1913 IT HAD ABOUT 160 SEMI-HANDICRAFT INDUSTRIES EMPLOYING 14,500 WORKERS IN ALL. TODAY THERE ARE ABOUT 500 PLANTS IN KIEV, AMONG THEM THE HUGE BOLSHEVIK MACHINE-BUILDING WORKS, THE LENINSKAYA KUZNITSA SHIPYARDS, AND THE GORKY MACHINE TOOL PLANT IN SVYATOSHINO. KIEV ALREADY HAS SOME 100,000 WORKERS. THE DAMAGE OF WAR AND CIVIL WAR HAS BEEN REPAIRED AND MANY FINE BUILDINGS AND HOUSES HAVE BEEN ERECTED IN THESE PAST TWENTY YEARS.

KIEV IS THE HEART AND BRAIN OF THE UKRAINE. IT IS THE HEADQUARTERS OF THE POLITICAL STAFF OF THE REPUBLIC—THE CENTRAL COMMITTEE OF THE COMMUNIST PARTY OF THE UKRAINE, AND OF THE SUPREME SOVIET AND COUNCIL OF PEOPLE'S COMMISSARS OF THE UKRAINIAN SOVIET SOCIALIST REPUBLIC.

IT IS THE SEAT OF THE UKRAINIAN ACADEMY OF SCIENCES WITH ITS NUMEROUS SCIENTIFIC RESEARCH INSTITUTES.

THE KIEV THEATRES ARE THE FINEST IN THE UKRAINE AND RANK WITH THE BEST IN THE SOVIET UNION, AND MANY OF THEIR ACTORS AND ACTRESSES HAVE BEEN RECIPIENTS OF ORDERS, THE HIGHEST DISTINCTIONS OF THE UNION.

WITH ITS MAGNIFICENT PARKS AND GARDENS AND SPACIOUS SQUARES AND AVENUES, KIEV IS A CITY THAT COMMANDS OUR ADMIRATION.

TODAY IT HAS A POPULATION OF 850,000, BUT WITHIN EIGHT OR TEN YEARS THIS FIGURE WILL HAVE GROWN TO SOME ONE AND A HALF MILLION.

NEW DISTRICTS WILL BE BUILT. IT WILL BE GIRDLED BY A DOUBLE BELT OF PARKS AND GREEN AVENUES, ONE WITHIN THE CITY, FOLLOWING THE BANKS OF THE DNIEPER, AND ONE AROUND THE CITY BOUNDARY.

A PARK OF CULTURE AND RECREATION WILL BE LAID OUT ON THE BLUFFS OVERLOOKING THE DNIEPER.

MAGNIFICENT KIEV WILL BE THRICE MAGNIFICENT!

AND THIS SOUTHERN CITY, SO BUSTLING AND ACTIVE, SO SUAVE AND GAY IN HOLIDAY MOOD, YET SO MENACING IN DAYS OF POPULAR WRATH, THIS CITY, WHICH HAS SUFFERED SO MUCH AT THE HANDS OF THE BUTCHERS OF THE UKRAINIAN PEOPLE, YET IS SO QUICK TO RECOVER AND SO EAGER FOR NEW LIFE, IS LOVED NOT ONLY BY ITS OWN INHABITANTS AND BY THE INHABITANTS OF THE UKRAINE; IT IS LOVED BY EVERY SOVIET PATRIOT, WHETHER IN BYELORUSSIA OR IN GEORGIA, IN MOSCOW OR IN THE FAR EAST. KIEV IS PRIZED BY ALL THE NATIONS OF THE GREAT SOVIET UNION. AND WHOEVER DARES RAISE HIS HAND AGAINST THE SOVIET UKRAINE AND ITS SPLENDID CAPITAL WILL BE CRUSHED BY THE FULL MIGHT OF THE SOCIALIST STATE.

THE SOVIET PAVILION OF THE ARCTIC

Nearly two hundred years ago the Russian scientist and poet, Lomonosov, wrote: "Russian Columbuses . . . will open a gate through ice and link our mighty nation with America." This has been realized in the Soviet era. Soviet explorers, scientists, seamen, aviators and workers have converted the Arctic into a navigable seaway, and are making immense areas within the Arctic Circle habitable.

The story of this modern epic of exploration and pioneering is told in the displays in the Pavilion of the Arctic. Before the pavilion stands the plane in which Valery Chkalov made the first transpolar flight from Moscow to the United States; inside is the actual hut and equipment used by the Papanin Expedition which made scientific observations for nine months on a North Pole ice floe. On the ceiling, on an illuminated map, the routes of the historic transpolar flights of Chkalov and Gromov, the recent flight of Kokkinaki from Moscow to America, and the route of the Papanin drift are shown. Additional exhibits record other heroic episodes and the vast scientific, industrial, and cultural progress in the Soviet Arctic.

UNION OF SOVIET SOCIALIST REPUBLICS

NEW YORK
WORLD'S FAIR 1939

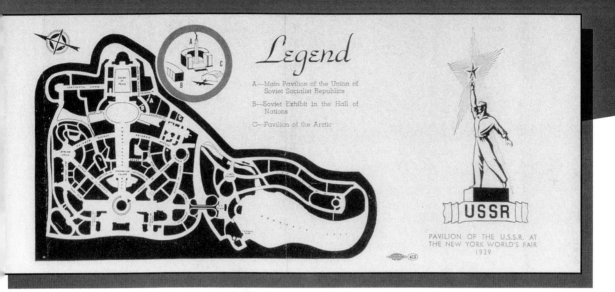

Legend

A—Main Pavilion of the Union of Soviet Socialist Republics

B—Soviet Exhibit in the Hall of Nations

C—Pavilion of the Arctic

PAVILION OF THE U.S.S.R. AT THE NEW YORK WORLD'S FAIR 1939

It was the spring of 1939, and all seemed right with the world-- assuming one didn't glance over toward Europe. So why not invite the U.S.S.R. to open a pavilion at the New York World's Fair? In fact, why not let them have *three*? So, as you see here, Russia was represented by the Arctic Pavilion and the Main Pavilion of the U.S.S.R., in addition to the Soviet exhibit in the Hall of Nations. This sort of ruthless expansionism should have tipped us off as to Stalin's true intentions toward Poland and Finland, but everyone at the Fair must have been too busy queuing up for the Parachute Jump and ogling the nearly naked mermaids at Billy Rose's Aquacade. That's why they call it *decadent* capitalism.

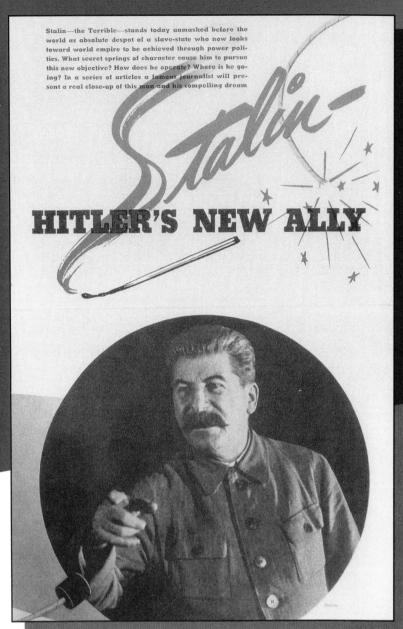

Stalin—

HITLER'S NEW ALLY

News of the Hitler-Stalin Pact of August 1939 was not well received by the American media. Consider the response of that esteemed journal of political theory, *Cosmopolitan*, which quickly prepared this vituperative piece on Stalin the Terrible, "Stalin--Hitler's New Ally," for its November issue:

It has taken the biggest diplomatic bombshell of this generation--the announcement of a virtual alliance between Russia and Germany on the very edge of the war volcano--to make the world see the obvious. Stalin, who already has a stranglehold on one-sixth of the earth's habitable surface in his own country, is reaching out cautiously, systematically, for dominion beyond his own frontiers. That is the hard core of meaning in recent events.

As Hitler's double-cross fluttered beside Stalin's hammer and sickle in Moscow, even the most deluded recognized the sinister outlines of some towering truths long familiar to realistic students of the one-man show in the Kremlin . . . . The world in 1939 still thinks it is dealing with the Russia of 1919. That Russia is dead. The change that has come over it is admitted occasionally with extraordinary candor by the new-style Communists themselves. Months ago the Soviet Ambassador in London, Ivan Maisky, said: "We are not sentimentalists like you. We are thinking only of Russia, not of humanity."

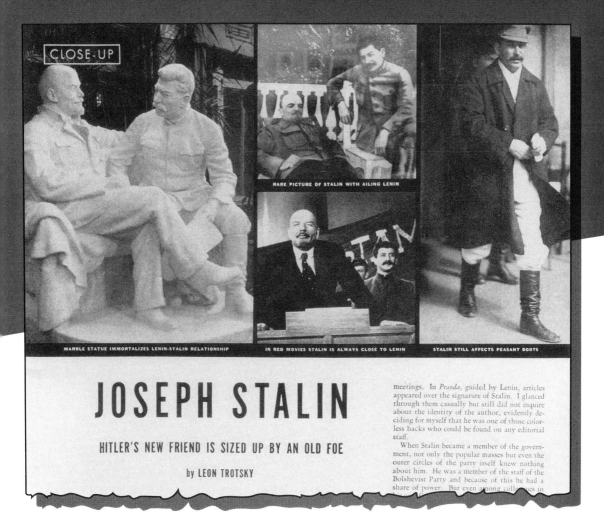

CLOSE-UP

RARE PICTURE OF STALIN WITH AILING LENIN

MARBLE STATUE IMMORTALIZES LENIN-STALIN RELATIONSHIP   IN RED MOVIES STALIN IS ALWAYS CLOSE TO LENIN   STALIN STILL AFFECTS PEASANT BOOTS

JOSEPH STALIN

HITLER'S NEW FRIEND IS SIZED UP BY AN OLD FOE

by LEON TROTSKY

meetings. In *Pravda*, guided by Lenin, articles appeared over the signature of Stalin. I glanced through them casually but still did not inquire about the identity of the author, evidently deciding for myself that he was one of those colorless hacks who could be found on any editorial staff.

When Stalin became a member of the government, not only the popular masses but even the outer circles of the party itself knew nothing about him. He was a member of the staff of the Bolshevist Party and because of this he had a share of power. But even among colleagues in

The October 2, 1939, issue of *Life* contained a more measured essay on Stalin by none other than his old foe Leon Trotsky. "Joseph Stalin" is surprisingly devoid of bitterness; indeed, its tone is gently mocking, as Stalin is pictured hugging peasant children and reflectively lighting his pipe. (As if the beleaguered fellow could have possibly anticipated today's breakthroughs in public relations!) "Both Stalin and Hitler have little respect for treaties," Trotsky observes. "How long will a treaty between them endure?" About twenty-two months, as it turned out.

Even during the years of the Hitler-Stalin Pact, when a good part of the print media in America was dusting off its old Red Scare files, Hollywood remained fairly sanguine about our relationship with the Soviet Union. M-G-M's *Ninotchka* ("The Picture That Kids the Commissars!") went into production in 1939 before the non-aggression pact changed the world alignment, but it still charmed audiences when it was released on November 10. This frothy tale of an icy apparatchik (Garbo in one of her best roles) who has been sent to Paris to discipline a group of Soviet trade representatives who have been seduced by the charms of the West, only to fall in love herself with a decadent capitalist (Melvyn Douglas), is now recognized as a classic of romantic comedy. In fact, *Ninotchka* was nominated for several Academy Awards in that most stellar of Hollywood years, including Best Picture, Best Actress (Garbo), Best Original Story, and Best Screenplay. Hardly the sort of reception one might have expected during a time when Red-baiting was in bloom. (Interestingly, the film was rereleased in 1948 and again in 1962, both periods of intense Cold War activity.)

Photofest

M-G-M was so pleased with the success of *Ninotchka* that it virtually remade the film in 1940, in the form of the less effervescent *Comrade X*. Here it is Clark Gable who assumes the role of the irresistible Westerner, with Hedy Lamarr as the frigid Russian who inevitably melts before Gable's All-American ardor. Lamarr plays a streetcar conductor whose heretical Communistic "purity" is about to get her purged by the Party. Gable, a Moscow-based newspaperman, is coerced by Lamarr's father into smuggling her out of the country to safety. Gable pretends to be a Communist himself who needs Lamarr to help him spread propaganda in the States. But the secret police arrest the pair and condemn them to death, a fate they avert when Gable steals a tank which Hedy drives to freedom. Unlikely? You bet. But this bizarre combination of screwball comedy and two-fisted adventure still won an Oscar nomination for screenwriter Walter Reisch, who had cowritten *Ninotchka* and years later would attempt another version of the story with *The Iron Petticoat* (1956).

But even such mild criticisms of Mother Russia would soon become dormant in Hollywood in less than a year, when Hitler and Stalin obtained a divorce and the Soviets suddenly became our dearly loved brethren.

THE "TROJAN HORSE" POLICY OF COMMUNISM IN AMERICA

COMMUNISM is the greatest menace to the domestic peace of the United States today. For three reasons: The virus of its democracy-wrecking disease is not easily recognized by laymen who often mistake it for liberalism. The American Communist Party is so potently organized and politically powerful that it exerts an influence which out-proportions its actual numbers. A foothold already has been gained in colleges, labor, relief and even hospitals. This is a result of the new "Trojan-horse" policy adopted in Moscow, 1935. The expressed purpose was to penetrate—within democracies—"every organization which might put Communists in places of influence." Greatest success of such "penetration" to date is with the Workers' Alliance, organization of the unemployed and WPA workers. Prominent among the Reds who dictate their policies is Secretary-Treasurer Herbert Benjamin, admittedly a Communist for 18 years. With such leadership the Alliance remains a government-supported organization alien to democratic principles . . . a club to batter not only the government that feeds it, but the already over-burdened taxpayers who pay for the food.

Wide World

FROM this ninth floor office, 50 E. 13th Street, New York City, Browder directs the activities of 75,000 American Communists. For each card-carrying member there are said to be 15 to 20 "sympathizers."

Acme

A "RED-HUNT" by Atty.-Gen. A. Mitchell Palmer in 1919 squelched the party until 1923.

International

AN ALLEGED Communist is arrested during a 1930 Labor Day clash with the "cossacks." Civil warfare has been stopped by edict of party leaders.

A bargain-basement competitor to *Life* and *Look* magazines, *Click* debuted in 1938--the same year the House Un-American Activities Committee was founded. Coincidence? Perhaps. But as these two rabid *Click* essays--"The 'Trojan Horse' Policy of Communism in America" (September 1939) and "If the Communists Seized America in 1942" (March 1940)--indicate, some Americans didn't have to wait for the arrival of Joe McCarthy to be whipped into an anti-Red frenzy.

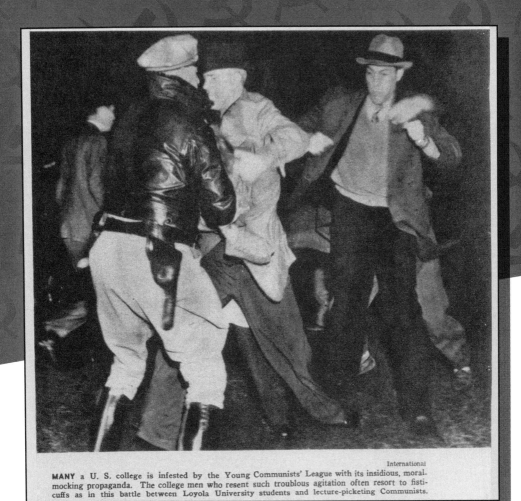

MANY a U. S. college is infested by the Young Communists' League with its insidious, moral-mocking propaganda. The college men who resent such troublous agitation often resort to fisti-cuffs as in this battle between Loyola University students and lecture-picketing Communists.

"The 'Trojan Horse' Policy," published within weeks of the Stalin-Hitler Pact, was a five-alarm blaze of rhetoric, from its opening salvo--"Communism is the greatest menace to the domestic peace of the United States today"--to its montage of photographs showing Reds peacefully demonstrating, engaging in sit-down strikes, and participating in hunger marches. (The godless fiends!) Their photo of the dumpy CP headquarters in New York City, though, tended to undercut the anonymous writer's panicky predictions of an imminent takeover by the Commies.

IF THE COMMUNISTS SEIZED AMERICA IN 1942—

A FORMER PARTY LEADER REVEALS THE RED PROGRAM FOR FOMENTING REVOLUTION IN THE UNITED STATES

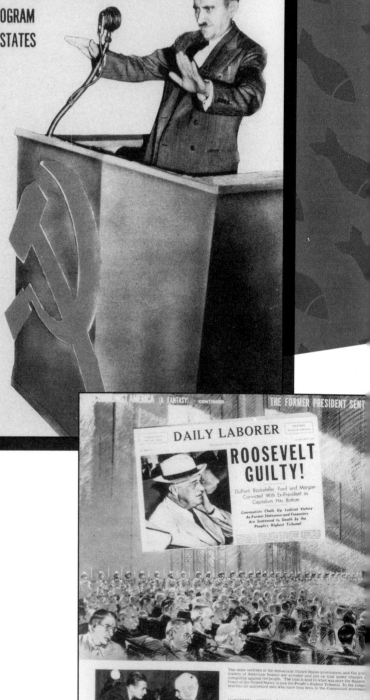

A FANTASY by BEN GITLOW

A leading light in the Communist Labor Party and the Workers' (Communist) Party, antecedents of the present Communist Party of the United States, which expelled him, Ben Gitlow should be well qualified to expose the true nature of the Communist program in U. S. CLICK prints his fantasy as an interesting document, without endorsing the author's opinions.

IN 1942 the Communists succeeded in overthrowing the Government of the United States. This is how it came about.

Franklin D Roosevelt had been elected for a third term. The war in Europe had spread to the Balkans, to the Scandinavian countries; Holland and Belgium were invaded and the world was caught in a conflagration that threatened the destruction of civilization. The totalitarian powers, Germany and Russia, were desperately attempting to bring down in ruins Western civilization, in an effort to establish their hegemony over the world. The Communist International was arousing the peoples of Asia and Africa against British and French imperialism. The United States was included in the imperialist block. Nazi and Communist agents in Latin America, in the Philippines and wherever the United States exerted influence, were busily engaged in fomenting opposition to Yankee imperialism. American trade was interfered with, American property in Latin America seized and American interests in foreign countries threatened. Conditions forced the Roosevelt administration to adopt the unpopular course of entering the war.

The people were divided in their approval of the country's entrance into the war. The progress of the war played right into the hands of the Communists. They represented themselves as the spearhead of the opposition to the war. Unable to achieve the unity necessary for a successful prosecution of the war, attacked on all sides by the Nazi and Communist forces on the one hand and the genuine

DAILY LABORER

ROOSEVELT GUILTY!

DuPont, Rockefeller, Ford and Morgan Convicted With Ex-President as Capitalism Hits Bottom

Communists Chalk Up Judicial Victory As Former Statesmen and Financiers Are Sentenced to Death by the People's Highest Tribunal

The once-servers of the democratic United States government and the great leaders of American finance are arrested and put on trial under charges of conspiring against the people. The trial is held in what was once the Supreme Court of the United States, is now the People's Highest Tribunal. In the rising benches sit uniformed men who have long been in the Communist movement.

(continued) greatest American liberator, a combination of George Washington, Thomas Jefferson and Abraham Lincoln. Little did they realize that Browder had nothing to do with guiding the destiny of the country but that every step made by the Communist Party and its leadership was determined by Stalin's agents of the Comintern. The people, however, were inspired with the belief that America was starting a new course The bankers, the Wall street manipulators, the industrial magnates, all of them—including the Morgans, the DuPonts, the Fords and the Rockefellers, had been swept into oblivion by the current of the revolution. Now the poor people expected to rule.

The workers and farmers of America were told they were masters of their own destiny. The new government, was to bring peace. Planned economy was to provide the people with an abundance of the good things in life, and the people would enjoy an era of prosperity and happiness.

The new government was patterned after the Russian Soviet. It decreed that only one party, the Communist Party, would function. All other political parties were outlawed. Among these, in addition to the Republican and Democratic parties, were the several Socialist parties, and the Anarchists. The most ruthless campaign of extermination was conducted against the small Com

DEATH AFTER GIGANTIC MASS TRIAL

in America, many of them served jail sentences under the old regime. The deposed President is standing to hear the sentence of the court: Death. Later four co-defendants, DuPont, Rockefeller, Ford and Morgan (left foreground) hear the same judgment. Red soldiers line the walls. Although no cameras were allowed, an artist made this sketch for the Party press (see inset).

munist opposition groups, the Trotskyites and Lovestoneites. By this act, political democracy was categorically destroyed.

The Constitution of the United States was replaced by a constitution which followed in detail every provision of the Constitution of the Soviet Union, and ignored the political traditions of American democracy. The government and the Communist Party took over all newspapers, all publications, theatres, production of movies, news gathering agencies, radio stations. The Communists obtained a stranglehold on all public opinion and cultural activities.

Most of the officials and representatives of the United States Government had been arrested

and executed during the course of the revolutionary uprising. President Roosevelt was the central figure of a dramatic mass trial. He was charged with being in the employ of the international bankers and munition manufacturers, conspiring to push the country into the war. All were found guilty and sentenced to death.

The trade unions were converted into government agencies supervised by Communist politicians who enforced all the decrees and rules of the government pertaining to labor and production, especially the ban on strikes.

The American f a r m e r s were soon to learn that the Communists, who showed so much concern over the farmers' plight, before *(story continued on next page)*

Also massive, although not sentenced to death, would be Labor Leader John L. Lewis (right), for the Communists fear his influence with the workers. Political commentators who condemn Communism, like Hugh Johnson, (left) would be quietly rubbed out.

CONTINUED ON NEXT PAGE

"If the Communists Seized America in 1942" was even more fun. This "fantasy" is credited to Ben Gitlow, a self-avowed "former leader of the American Communist movement" who makes no bones about the chances for a peaceful revolution in America. "I have not met a single Communist who did not agree that (it) would be a revolution of bullets--not ballots," Gitlow confides. "Lenin laid down the Communist position when he wrote, 'The replacement of the bourgeois by the proletarian state is impossible without a violent revolution.'" True. But the utter lunacy of the accompanying illustration convinces me that the article was actually ghost-written by J. Edgar Hoover himself. Who else could so gleefully have fantasized FDR being sentenced to death by a Red tribunal? The accuracy of Gitlow's predictions could not, alas, be tested; by 1942, the U.S.S.R.--now under attack from Hitler--would be our most cherished ally.

In America, one of the most visible aftereffects of Operation Barbarossa--the code name for Hitler's 1941 strike against the Soviet Union--was how quickly and wholeheartedly Hollywood supported the cause of the U.S.S.R. Beginning in 1942, when such documentaries as *Battle of Russia* and *Our Russian Front* ("SEE the heroism of men and women fighting on our side!") were hastily assembled using war footage, Americans were treated to an unremitting stream of tales about Our Valiant Allies. And why not? They hated Hitler, and so did we. For less compelling reasons are alliances often forged. So, while FDR was pledging a billion dollars of Lend-Lease support, Hollywood leapt in with its own contributions. Some were B-pictures like *Miss V from Moscow* and *Three Russian Girls*, which used the war as background for formulaic romances with a light sprinkling of pro-Russian propaganda. Others were based on more specific historial situations. Fox's 1943 entry, *Chetniks*, dramatized the struggle of a brave group of Yugoslav partisans who battle and ultimately outwit their Nazi occupiers. Inspiring stuff, except that in reality General Mihajlovic's Chetniks tended to collaborate with the Nazis, the better to wage their own war against Tito's Communist guerrillas. Better still, Columbia's *The Boy from Stalingrad*, also 1943, showed the youth of Russia whipping the bejeezus out of the Nazis.

And then there was *Mission to Moscow.* A best-selling book when published in 1941, the film version of Ambassador Joseph Davies' adventures while stationed in Moscow from 1936 to 1938 was brought to the screen by Warner Brothers in 1943. Described by film historian Nora Sayre as a "gigantic mashnote to our ally," *Mission to Moscow* softened the book's already tolerant account of Stalin during the purge years into something approaching hagiography. The Moscow trials of 1937 and 1938 are shown as being conducted with the genial goodwill of the courtroom scene in *Mr. Deeds Goes to Town*, and Stalin is presented as a visionary who was driven into Hitler's arms by the dimwittedness of the British and French (which was at least partly the case). At one point, the Davies character, played by the estimable Walter Huston, tells Stalin, "I believe, sir, that history will record you as a great benefactor of mankind"-- a line that does not appear in the book. But Davies himself appears in the film's prologue, praising "those fine and patriotic citizens," the Warner brothers, thus indicating he wasn't too upset by the liberties taken in adapting his book. *Mission to Moscow* ends with a heavenly apparition who asks, "Am I my brother's keeper?" as disembodied voices answer, "Yes, you are--now and forever more!"

Forever didn't last too long, though. By 1947 the House Un-American Activities Committee was asking Jack Warner to explain how such shamefully pro-Soviet propaganda could have come from his studio. Had FDR made a personal appeal? Had the government helped subsidize the production? Warner answered in the negative, though he changed his story in his 1965 autobiography: there he says yes, the President had made just such a request, "and I considered FDR's request an order." Unfortunately, this revelation came far too late to save the career of screenwriter Howard Koch, who was blacklisted, in large part because of his work on *Mission to Moscow*. As film critic James Agee noted at the time, "the film is almost describable as the first Soviet production to come from a major American studio."

Scenes from THE NORTH STAR

Early in 1944, two films were released that matched *Mission to Moscow*'s ardor for the heroism of the Soviet Union. M-G-M's *Song of Russia*, adapted from a property called *Scorched Earth*, and *The North Star*, made by the Goldwyn studio from an original story by Lillian Hellman, both left Stalin himself out of the picture while pouring on the pathos for the plight of the peasantry.

 Set in the summer of 1941, *The North Star* opens with a family of jolly Russians sitting at their humble breakfast table. But their banter is brought to a sudden halt by a report that comes over the radio: *"One hundred and twelve Polish children died yesterday as a result of forced blood transfusions to the German wounded."* The news of this atrocity outrages the peasants, especially the father of the clan (Walter Huston), who is a doctor. Still, that evening the communal picnic goes off as planned, with the young lovers (Farley Granger and Anne Baxter), the jovial pilot (Dana Andrews, smiling for the first and last time in his film career), and the other villagers joining in song. Then the Nazis invade the town. Led by the pitiless Dr. Van Herden (Erich von Stroheim, in a classic performance), the German soldiers extinguish the fires the villagers had set as part of the scorched-earth approach to denying the invaders food and habitation. As punishment for their defiance, the Nazis select a woman from the crowd and break an arm and a leg.

SAMUEL GOLDWYN'S MASTERPIECE...

"THE NORTH STAR"

But several villagers escape, and join the guerrilla forces. "The earth belongs to us, the people, if we fight for it--and we will fight for it!" is their cry. In the meantime, the Nazis have segregated the children of the village and are using them for blood transfusions to aid their wounded. When a child dies from the procedure, von Stroheim apologizes to fellow doctor Huston--but Huston bides his time, and has the pleasure of shooting him in cold blood in a climactic showdown. By film's end, Dana Andrews has died making a kamikaze attack on a German supply line, Farley Granger has been blinded, and the guerrillas have staged a brilliant tactical attack to recapture the village and defeat the Nazis.

"Strictly speaking, The North Star is not a war picture," the film's promotional booklet explained. "Mr. Goldwyn has sent a camera into a Soviet village to introduce to America a people much like ourselves, to explain in terms of entertainment the source of the Russians' strength."

Hokey but in the end rousing, the film was given Look's coveted cover slot in January of 1944. But by 1947, when the film was rereleased as Armored Attack, things had changed so drastically that most of the shots of friendly village life were trimmed, leaving a war story devoid of propaganda. Even at that, a prologue explaining that the Russians "used to be" our ally was deemed necessary. A wise decision, with HUAC waiting in the wings.

Song of Russia was a typically glitzy production from M-G-M. Robert Taylor plays a famous American conductor who is touring the Soviet Union before the war breaks out. One of his Russian fans, played by Susan Peters, manages to meet him and wrangle a fancy dinner out of him. Taylor falls for her when he realizes that she's "just like an American girl." Amid much Tchaikovsky, the young lovers visit her parents' farm, where Peters wows the conductor by repairing tools and driving a tractor. Smitten, Taylor marries her in a local church, but the honeymoon is interrupted by the Nazi invasion. Peters sets about making Molotov cocktails, and (true to the film's source) helps set the town ablaze so the invaders cannot use its resources. *Song of Russia* ends with Taylor and Peters being sent to America to tell us, "We are soldiers, side by side, in this fight for all humanity." (Donations to Russian War Relief, Inc., gratefully accepted.)

Photofest

Screenwriter Richard Collins testified before HUAC in April 1951 that *Song of Russia* had seemed "pretty innocuous" to him and cowriter Paul Jarrico--both of Communist leanings--but that star Robert Taylor had objected to the pro-Russia slant, leading to the deletion of all references to collective farms and the like. Producer David Selznick refused to lend Ingrid Bergman to the project because the script he saw was too favorable to Russia, which mystified M-G-M head Louis B. Mayer, who "just wanted to make a picture about Russia, not Communists." Collins--who named twenty-three names before the Committee--concluded that *Song of Russia* "was actually pretty lukewarm" in relation to American popular support of the U.S.S.R. at that time.

But writer Ayn Rand, a virulent anti-Communist, told HUAC that the film made her "sick," and that all the smiling of the peasants throughout was totally unrealistic. (What? *You* wouldn't grin while throwing a Molotov cocktail at a Nazi parachuter?) Robert Taylor, another friendly witness, testified that he only agreed to appear in the movie because the Office of War Information had pressured M-G-M to make it. He must not have heard the slogan of the Communist Political Association: "Communism *Is* Twentieth-Century Americanism."

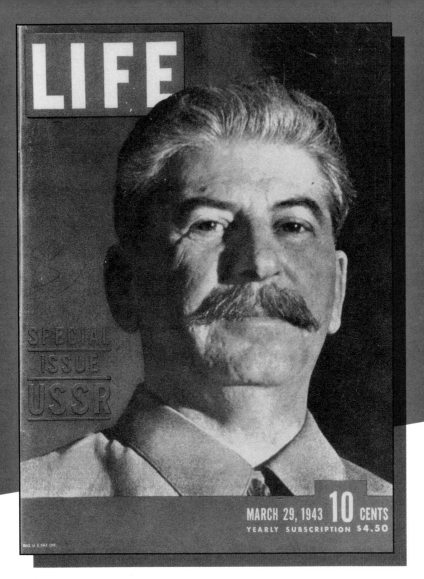

LIFE

SPECIAL ISSUE U.S.S.R

MARCH 29, 1943 **10** CENTS
YEARLY SUBSCRIPTION $4.50

REG. U.S. PAT. OFF.

One of the most formidable efforts to acquaint Americans with their Soviet soulmates was the March 29, 1943, issue of *Life* magazine. This massive undertaking opened with a somber cover shot of Stalin (was there any other kind?) by Margaret Bourke-White and proceeded through over a hundred pages of articles, charts, and photo-essays "portraying the works and manners of the Russian people." In a lengthy letter to their readers, *Life*'s editors justified the existence of the project:

> We have done this issue for one chief reason. There are two ways by which nations can come close together; one is through their State Departments, the other is through popular sympathy and understanding. The editors of LIFE can't do anything about the U.S. State Department. We can, however, help our readers to see and understand the Russian people. And we'd like to think that maybe Russian journalists will undertake a similar project about the U.S.
>
> Of course, the Russians don't entirely agree with this idea. They live under a system of tight state-controlled information. But probably the attitude to take toward this is not to get too excited about it. When we take account of what the U.S.S.R. has accomplished in the 20 years of its existence we can make allowances for certain shortcomings, however deplorable . . . .

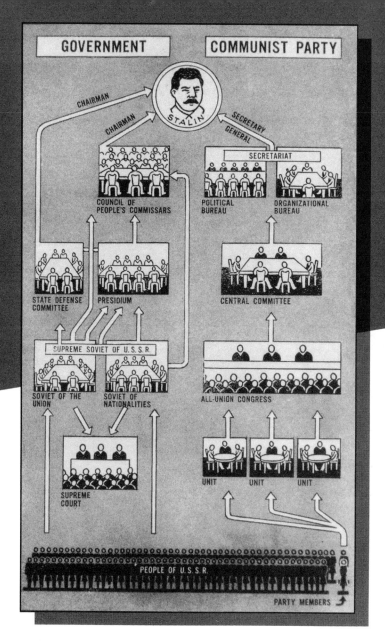

Among the articles in this special issue were "Lenin, Father of Modern Russia," "Russians Like Athletics," "Peoples of the U.S.S.R." (all 175 different nationalities duly noted), "Life of a Ballet Performer," and "Collective Farms Feed the Nation." There was also a close-up of "Red Leaders," and an elaborate history entitled "One Thousand Years of Russia." But the key piece was "The Soviets of the Post-War," by Joseph E. Davies, of *Mission to Moscow* fame. Our ambassador to the U.S.S.R. from 1936 to 1938, Davies allays any lingering suspicions of the Soviets by answering, in reassuring fashion, questions like "Is Russia determined to pursue the cause of world revolution?" (Gosh, I doubt it!) and "Can we assume that the rulers of Russia are men of goodwill toward other nations?" (I'd bet the farm!).

Whether the editors of *Life* were purged--or merely reeducated--once Stalin was no longer America's poster boy, can only be speculated upon. But judging from the jingoistic journalism the magazine indulged in during the Cold War, it is safe to assume that no proposals for a second special issue on the U.S.S.R. were ever entertained by *Life*'s editorial board.

The prewar Stalin, in tunic, with wide, curving mustache, approves the record of two Tadjikistan farmer girls. Right

A Guy Named Joe

He knows Arctic meteorology, *Leatherstocking Tales*, soap, and war

By RALPH PARKER

Moscow correspondent for Overseas Press, New York Times, London *Times;* co-author of *The Last Days of Sevastopol*

The human side of "Uncle Joe" Stalin, as presented by *Look* magazine in its issue of June 27, 1944. According to writer Ralph Parker, a correspondent based in Moscow, Stalin spent half his time writing poetry and the other half reading it to the schoolchildren who flocked to sit on his knee. (Ambassador Joseph Davies also remarked on Stalin's kindly way with children, in his book *Mission to Moscow*.) Noting that "Stalin is undoubtedly among the best-dressed of all world leaders, [making] Churchill in his siren suit look positively shabby," Parker goes on to sketch the literary interests of Russia's fearsome--yet sensitive--leader:

" Perhaps there is a clue to this all-round knowledge in Stalin's school certificate on exhibit in the Tiflis Museum. It establishes that Josif Vissarionovich Dzhugashvili made top marks in all subjects except Greek.

In addition to this man of trenchant speech, indomitable will and extraordinary mental capacity, there is another Stalin--the lover of literature. A Stalin who will suddenly ask an engineer if he read Fenimore Cooper as a boy--Stalin did. A Stalin who at age 16 was writing poetry; who--even during the war--is deeply concerned with the work of younger poets, playwrights, novelists, eager that they should express the new Russia's soul.

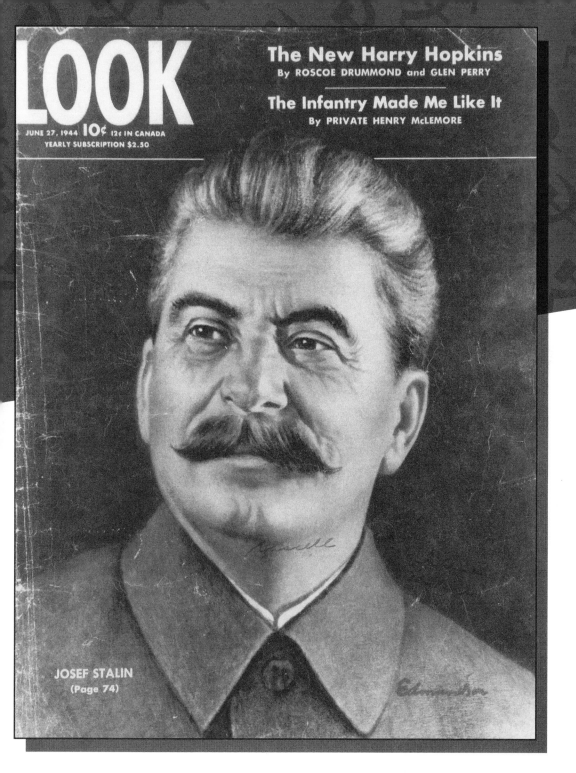

LOOK

JUNE 27, 1944 10¢ 12¢ IN CANADA
YEARLY SUBSCRIPTION $2.50

The New Harry Hopkins
By ROSCOE DRUMMOND and GLEN PERRY

The Infantry Made Me Like It
By PRIVATE HENRY McLEMORE

JOSEF STALIN
(Page 74)

"'A Guy Named Joe' also makes the point that, before the war, Marshal Stalin handled problems on the level of choosing the 'most suitable' wrapping for a bar of soap. The implication is clear: as soon as this damned war is over, Stalin will return to reading *The Deerslayer* and polishing his verse. Somehow, it never happened. Perhaps feeling betrayed, *Look* would soon emerge as one of the most tireless Stalin-bashers in the American press, while Parker, presumably, was placed under house arrest for disseminating pro-Joe propaganda."

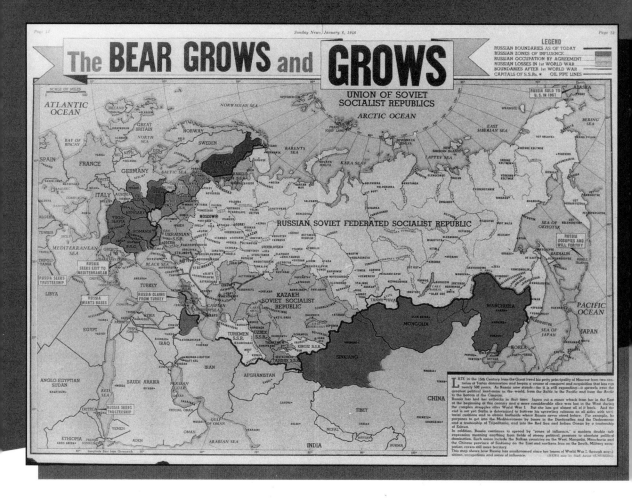

Presented as the centerfold of the Sunday magazine section of the New York *Daily News* on January 6, 1946, "The Bear Grows and Grows" illustrated America's dawning perception that the U.S.S.R. was a mighty large and hungry nation, one whose borders were constantly moving outward. The Yalta agreement of February 1945 had already given the signal that the Soviets were in an expansionist mood, now that the Germans were off their backs for the first time in five years. Stalin's appetite for acquisition was already a matter of record; after all, it had been his bold (some would say foolhardy) annexation of Bessarabia from Romania in June of 1940 that had effectively forced Hitler to terminate the non-aggression pact and invade Russia.

LATE in the 15th Century Ivan the Great freed his petty principality of Moscow from two centuries of Tartar domination and began a course of conquest and acquisition that has run nearly 500 years. As Russia now stands—for it is still expanding—it sprawls over the greatest political land-mass in the world, from the Baltic to the Pacific and from the Arctic to the bottom of the Caspian.

Russia has had her setbacks in that time: Japan cut a minor whack from her in the East at the beginning of this century and a more considerable slice was lost in the West during the complex struggles after World War I. But she has got almost all of it back. And the end is not yet: Stalin is determined to buttress his sprawling colossus on all sides with territorial cushions and to obtain footholds where Russia never stood before. For example, he purposes to get into the Mediterranean by bases in the Dardanelles and the Dodecanese and a trusteeship of Tripolitania, and into the Red Sea and Indian Ocean by a trusteeship of Eritrea.

In addition, Russia continues to spread by "zones of influence," a modern double-talk expression meaning anything from fields of strong political pressure to absolute political domination. Such zones include the Balkan countries on the West, Mongolia, Manchuria and the Chinese province of Sinkiang on the East and northern Iran on the South. Military occupation covers still more territory.

This map shows how Russia has mushroomed since her losses of World War I, through acquisitions, occupations and zones of influence.   (NEWS map by Staff Artist SUNDBERG)

For the caption-writer of "The Bear Grows and Grows," the direction the postwar Soviet Union was taking was clear as a *Daily News* headline: "Stalin is determined to buttress his sprawling colossus on all sides with territorial cushions . . . . In addition, Russia continues to spread by 'zones of influence,' a modern double-talk expression meaning anything from fields of strong political pressure to absolute political domination." A few months later, Churchill would make his "Iron Curtain" speech at tiny Westminster College in Missouri, and the Cold War would officially commence.

LOOK FORUM QUESTION & ANSWER

A regular feature of *Look* magazine in the mid-forties, the "Look Forum" ran surprisingly frank answers from high-profile experts on the day's hot-potato questions. The sampling shown here appeared between November 1945 and May 1946. These exchanges illustrate how long it actually took for many Americans to realize that the honeymoon with Stalin was over, and that we were facing the dawn of a Cold War that would dominate our lives for the next twenty years. (To think that the question "Should we give the atomic bomb to Russia?" could actually be entertained late in 1945! . . .)

Do you believe we are at war with Russia now?

Rep. Helen G. Douglas (DEM., CAL.)
House Foreign Affairs Committee

No, I do not think that we are at war with Russia now. But too many people in the United States think we are, for a sound, peaceful relationship. The United States is the only nation in the world capable of making war at this time. Therefore the moral leadership the world needs is ours. Mrs. Clapper makes sense.

Chester Bowles
Ex-Director, Office of Economic Stabilization

Of course we are not at war with Russia. Moreover there is no earthly reason why we should fight Russia in the future. Both nations are fed up with war. Right now, both nations are insecure and suspicious. Through the U. N. a stable middle ground must be developed. In the meantime, what we need is less hysteria.

How can we avoid war with Russia?

By JOSEPH M. STACK
Commander-in-Chief, Veterans of Foreign Wars

Both the United States and Russia are committed to the principle that nations can settle all their differences without resorting to war, if they will seek an equitable solution in a spirit of co-operation, tolerance and respect for the rights of each other.

There are no points of conflict between our government and Russia's which cannot be settled on that principle. The mere suggestion of possible war with Russia is a grave threat to the program of international security and co-operation set forth in the United Nations charter. We can avoid war with Russia by putting an end to the attitude of fear and suspicion with which many have regarded every Russian move; and replacing it with an honest effort to better understand Russia's aims and policies.

Should we give the atomic bomb to Russia?

A By WILLIAM GREEN
President, American Federation of Labor

I am against giving the atomic-bomb secret to any nation. So long as the facilities for producing atomic bombs remain exclusively under our control, we know that world peace is safe and secure. Before the atomic-bomb secrets are shared with other nations, it is imperative that a much stronger international organization for world peace is effected. It is more important now than ever before that aggression be strongly outlawed, because in the future the first blow landed by a nation may end the war.

"STALIN THE STINKER!"

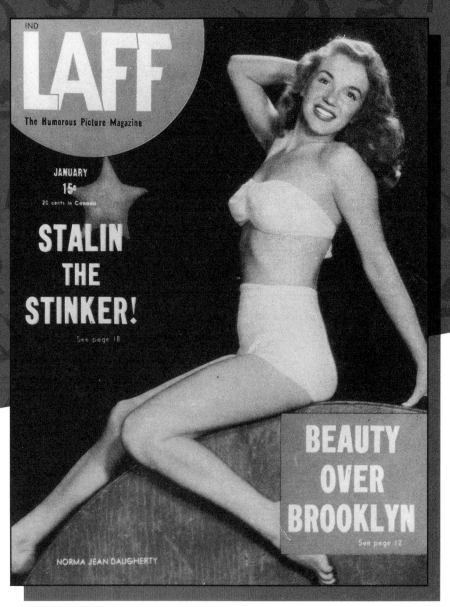

"To hell with Joe!" A sentiment perhaps shared by many Americans late in 1946, when this issue of *Laff* hit the newsstands, but not often voiced with such utter scorn--at least, not by the media at large. Not yet. But "Let's Not Be Moscow's Stooges!" does convey the attitude that would soon predominate, even in publications with more élan than the quasi-girlie magazine *Laff*.

And yes, that *is* a young Marilyn Monroe on the cover, working under the monicker Norma Jean Daugherty.

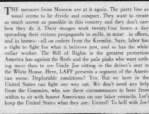

Stalin's a Stinker:
LET'S NOT BE MOSCOW'S STOOGES!

THE menaces from Moscow are at it again. The party line as usual seems to be divide and conquer. They want to create as much unrest as possible in this country and they don't care how they do it. Their stooges work twenty-four hours a day spreading their vicious propaganda in mills, in mine, in offices, and in homes—all on orders from the Kremlin. Sure, labor has a right to fight for what it believes just, and so has the white collar worker. The Bill of Rights is the greatest protection America has against the Reds and the pale pinks who want nothing more than to see Uncle Joe sitting in the driver's seat in the White House. Here, LAFF presents a segment of the American scene. Deplorable conditions? Yes. But we here in the United States can fight our way out. We don't need any help from the Commies, who use these circumstances to bore from within to sit with honest Americans on our labor councils. Let's keep the United States what they are: United! To hell with Joe!

A trucker's strike caused empty shelves in chain stores. And you can blame the Reds for keeping truckmen steamed up!

Tons of beef hang in strike-stopped packing houses. Commies know value of keeping people hungry—then they'll revolt!

Here's what happens when Americans fail to stick together and negotiate their differences. Joe likes these with his coffee!

Strikes can be settled without Red-inspired violence as these N. Y. truckmen showed during long and arduous negotiations.

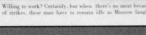

These Are Not Pleasant Pictures But They're What Every Communist Wants to See in These UNITED States

This is America, 1946. Red agitators have done a lot to foment strikes, keep American citizens like Chester Gillette homeless.

No coal. So thirty Illinois Central locomotives can't haul sorely-needed food and commodities to Americans, Mr. Lewis!

Willing to work? Certainly, but when there's no meat because of strikes, these men have to remain idle as Moscow laughs.

Anytime you find a black market, look for the Red-man in the picture. Here, Philadelphia crowds line up to buy butter!

HUAC

When the House Un-American Activities Committee (HUAC) was established in 1938, Congress empowered it to investigate any behavior that could be construed as unpatriotic. The vagueness of this assignment was much to the liking of Chairman Martin Dies of Texas, whom Harold Ickes described as "the outstanding zany of our generation." Dies was deeply disappointed when his search for Reds under every bed had to be temporarily sidetracked on account of the Nazi problem. His essay, "More Snakes Than I Can Kill," which appeared in *Liberty* magazine in 1940, and his book *The Trojan Horse in America* (ghostwritten by J. B. Matthews, author of *Odyssey of a Fellow Traveler*) are classics of the genre--or would be, if anyone remembered them. But Dies was replaced in 1945, and thus narrowly missed heading HUAC once the war's end permitted a quick and enthusiastic return to the ferreting out of crypto-Commies.

REDS ACTIVE IN HOLLYWOOD; BUT DIDN'T INFLUENCE FILMS

O'HARA SAYS INDUSTRY SUPPORTS RED HEARING

WAS RED BUT NOT NOW, PARKS SAYS

By 1947, the garland of headlines generated by HUAC's investigation into Hollywood's infiltration by Reds convinced that august body, now headed by New Jersey congressman J. Parnell Thomas, that there was gold in the Hollywood hills--and there they panned, and panned, and panned. A few of the nuggets they unearthed are illustrated on these pages: Gary Cooper being cute--and loyal--during his 1947 testimony; reports of screenwriter Richard Collins naming names, and a contrite Larry Parks confessing (but too late, his career was finished). Here, too, is the infamous *Red Channels*, the 1950 index to 151 blacklistable actors compiled by the ex-FBI agents who also brought you *Counterattack*, for the benefit of television and radio show sponsors (producers: ignore at your peril!). Thus were the tainted members of the broadcast and film communities thrown to the voracious wolves of HUAC.

"I'M NO COMMUNIST"

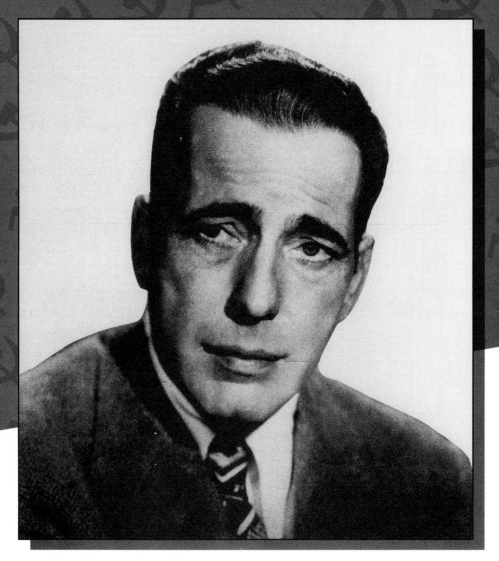

When Humphrey Bogart joined a contingent of fifty Hollywood directors, writers and actors bound for Washington, D.C., on a chartered plane to express their displeasure with the House Un-American Activities Committee's investigation into Communist infiltration of Hollywood, he must have felt nigh-invincible. At the peak of his popularity with the movie-going public, Bogart had starred in as many patriotic films during WWII as any actor in the land, including *Sahara*, *Action in the North Atlantic*, *To Have and Have Not*, and, of course *Casablanca*. What better icon of All-Americanism could the 300-member Committee for the First Amendment have chosen to lead the charge against HUAC's high-handed inquisition, spearheaded by the noxious J. Parnell Thomas? And so, on October 24, 1947, a bow-tied Bogie and a motley crew of film luminaries that included Lauren Bacall, Groucho Marx, Frank Sinatra, John Huston, Ronald Reagan, and Danny Kaye flew East to protect the rights of Alvah Bessie, Dalton Trumbo, Edward Dmytryk, Ring Lardner, Jr., John Howard Lawson, Lester Cole, Herbert Biberman, Albert Maltz, Adrian Scott, and Sam Ornitz--the "Hollywood Ten."

"Bad man" Bogie of "The Treasure of the Sierra Madre"

A plain-talking star answers his critics—and leaves no doubt about his meaning

BY HUMPHREY BOGART

Bogart and Bacall: "We're about as much in favor of Communism as J. Edgar Hoover"

A S the guy said to the warden, just before he was hanged: "This will teach me a lesson I'll never forget."

No, sir, I'll never forget the lesson that was taught to me in the year 1947, at Washington, D. C. When I got back to Hollywood, some friends sent me a mounted fish and underneath it was written: "If I hadn't opened my big mouth, I wouldn't be here."

The New York Times, the Herald Tribune and other reputable publications editorially had questioned the House Committee on Un-American Activities, warning that it was infringing on free speech. When a group of us Hollywood actors and actresses said the same thing, the roof fell in on us. In some fashion, I took the brunt of the attack. Suddenly, the plane that had flown us East became "Bogart's plane," carrying "Bogart's group." For once, top billing became embarrassing.

And the names that were called! Bogart, the capitalist, who always had loved his swimming pool, his fine home and all the other Hollywood luxuries, overnight had become Bogart, the Communist! Now there have been instances of miscasting, but this was the silliest. I refused to take it seriously, figuring that nobody else would take it seriously. The public, I figured, knew me and had known me for years. Sure, I had campaigned for FDR, but that had been the extent of my participation in politics. The public, I figured, must be aware of that and must be aware that not only was I completely American, but sincerely grateful for what the (Continued on page 86)

After stops and press conferences in Kansas City, St. Louis, and Chicago, Bogart's gang of fifty landed in Washington and held a press conference outside HUAC's very doors. But the effort was in vain. Not only would the uncooperative Hollywood Ten be cited for contempt of Congress and sent to prison (where, ironically, they were shortly joined by J. Parnell Thomas himself, who had been padding his payroll), but Bogart's own heroic image was tarnished by his high-profile defense of those impertinent subversives. Some hasty spin-control was called for, and Bogart rose--or descended--to the occasion with a press release describing himself as "a foolish and impetuous American" who detested Communism "just as any other decent American does." An expanded version of the statement appeared in the March 1948 issue of *Photoplay* magazine, concluding with Bogart's assessment of himself as a "dope."

Years later, Bogart would deny that he had ever made a retraction of his stance against HUAC. But Paul Henreid, Bogart's costar in *Casablanca*, labeled the statement "a form of betrayal," and renounced his friendship with Bogart. The "non-retraction" must have worked, though, because Bogart went on to win the 1952 Academy Award for Best Actor, while the Hollywood Ten had to work undercover for the next decade, when they could find work at all.

LOOK

VOLUME 11, NUMBER 5
MARCH 4, 1947

Earl Browder personifies the deep mysteries of Communism. He was an exalted leader when he made this speech; now he's in Party disgrace. Is it part of a plan?

How to Spot a Communist

Check before you sign that petition or join that little-known club; you might be supporting a secret cause

By LEO CHERNE

Executive Secretary, Research Institute of America

In a casual conversation at one of their historic meetings, President Roosevelt complained to Marshal Stalin about the behavior of American Communists. "They're not housebroken," he said.

"In my country," the Russian answered, "we know how to deal with opposition." Then he added: "They're your problem."

Stalin was right. The Communists are our problem. But his suggestion that they might be dealt with in the Russian way is not our answer. The American way is to argue them down, nail them on the facts and reveal them for what they are—the servants of a foreign power.

Nor was President Roosevelt quite frank in implying that the problem is one of manners. There is a real Communist problem in America.

Unfortunately, this problem is made more difficult by the reckless anti-Communist. The reckless anti-Communist is the person who calls everyone who disagrees with him a Communist. He carelessly lumps progressives, liberals, Socialists, atheists, world federationists, chronic dissenters and New Dealers under the Communist label. The result is that he throws up a smoke-screen behind which the real Communist can hide himself from attack.

The existence of the Communist as a real person, separate and distinct, must not be obscured by the shotgun barrage of a Dies or a Rankin committee. Nor should the red blanket which Hearst or Gerald L. K. Smith throws over all those who are against an ultra-conservative or a nationalist America be allowed to hide the real Communist from honest attack.

The real Communist is not a liberal or a progressive. He believes in Russia first and a Soviet America. He accepts the doctrines of dictatorship as practiced in Russia. And he is prepared to use a dictator's tactics of lies and violence to realize his ambitions.

Because the whole Communist apparatus is geared to secrecy, it is not always easy to determine just who is a Communist. But whether he is a Party card-holder or a fellow-traveler, the American Communist is not like other Americans. To the Communist, everything—his country, his job, his family—takes second place to his Party duty. Even his sex life is synchronized with the obligations of The Cause.

(Continued on next page) 21

How to Identify an American Communist

Adapted from material prepared by Friends of Democracy, Inc.

There is no simple definition of an American Communist. However, certain general classifications can be set up. And if either a person or an organization falls within most of these classifications, that person or organization can be said to be following the Communists' lead.

These identifying classifications include:

1 The belief that the war waged by Great Britain and her allies during the period from August, 1939, to June, 1941 (the period of the war before Russia was invaded), was an "imperialistic" war and a game of power politics.

2 The support of a foreign policy which agrees always with that followed by Soviet Russia, and which changes as the USSR policy changes.

3 The argument that any foreign or domestic policy which does not fit the Communist plan is advanced for ulterior motives and is not in the best interests of either the people or of world peace.

4 The practice of criticizing only American, British and Chinese policies, and never criticizing Soviet policies.

5 Continually receiving favorable publicity in such Communist publications as the *Daily Worker* and the *New Masses*.

6 Continually appearing as sponsor or co-worker of such known Communist-front groups as the Committee to Win the Peace, the Civil Rights Congress, the National Negro Congress and other groups which can be described as Communist inspired because they fall within the classifications set forth here.

7 Continually charging critics with being "Fascists," no matter whether the criticism comes from liberals, conservatives, reactionaries or those who really are Fascists.

8 Arguing for a class society by pitting one group against another; and putting special privileges ahead of community needs as, for example, claiming that labor has privileges but has no responsibilities in dealing with management.

9 Declaring that capitalism and democracy are "decadent" because some injustices exist under those systems.

Of course, actual membership in the Communist Party is 100 per cent proof, but this kind of proof is difficult to obtain.

Not bad, but we have our own Top Ten of "Ways to Spot a Commie" (circa 1947):

1. Keeps a pumpkin patch in his darkroom.

2. Doesn't click heels when J. Edgar Hoover drives past.

3. Cries whenever *Mission to Moscow* is shown at the neighborhood revival house.

4. Writes fan letters to Clifford Odets.

5. Plays handball with Earl Browder.

6. Thinks HUAC guys should attend Winter Carnival in Siberia.

7. Walks around with borscht stains on his tie.

8. Has a signed photograph of Molotov on his nightstand.

9. Prefers the crossword puzzles in *The Daily Worker* to *The Times'*.

10. Takes an extra-long lunch on May Day.

THE MOST AMAZING PLOT IN 3300 YEARS OF RECORDED ESPIONAGE!

DANA ANDREWS · GENE TIERNEY
in **THE IRON CURTAIN**

with JUNE HAVOC · BERRY KROEGER · EDNA BEST · STEFAN SCHNABEL · NICHOLAS JOY · EDUARD FRANZ · FREDERIC TOZÈRE

Directed by WILLIAM A. WELLMAN Produced by SOL C. SIEGEL Screen Play by Milton Krims

20th CENTURY FOX

Based on the Personal Story of Igor Gouzenko, Former Code Clerk, U.S.S.R. Embassy in Ottawa, Canada

THE IRON CURTAIN, the first Cold War film drawn from the headlines, dramatized the much-ballyhooed case of Igor Gouzenko, a code clerk at the Soviet Embassy in Ottawa, Canada. In 1945, he turned over to Canadian authorities 109 documents proving that his embassy coworkers had been stealing atomic secrets from the Allies. Eleven Soviet agents were convicted as a result of Gouzenko's efforts, most shockingly Fred Rose of the Canadian Parliament and scientist Alan Nunn May. Making good use of the phrase coined by Winston Churchill in his legendary 1946 speech ("From Stettin in the Baltic to Trieste in the Adriatic an iron curtain has descended across the Continent . . ."), 20th Century-Fox gave *The Iron Curtain* the full

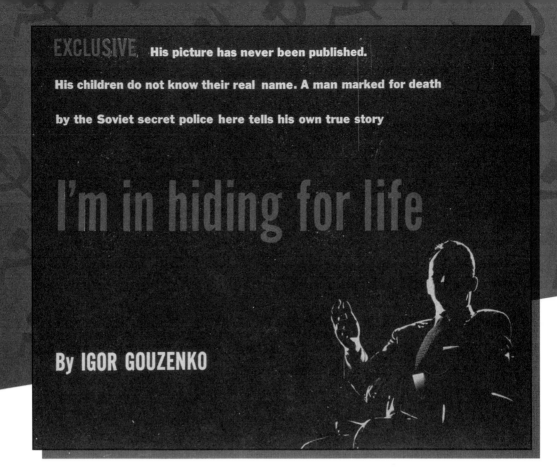

I'm in hiding for life

By IGOR GOUZENKO

A-picture treatment in 1948. Studio stars Dana Andrews and Gene Tierney were cast as Gouzenko and his wife Svetlana, and top director William Wellman was put in charge of the production. The result was a dark, almost dull account of Gouzenko's adventure, notable primarily for Andrews' perpetual pout. But *The Iron Curtain* did launch the cycle of Red Menace and A-spy films--that's A for atomic--that rolled into theaters like a Red tide over the next few years, most of which were considerably more fun than *The Iron Curtain.*

As for Gouzenko and his family, the Mounties put them into the Canadian version of the Witness Protection Program as a hedge against retaliation by the NKVD, the Soviet Union's far-flung secret police. (They were still very much on Gouzenko's mind, even after the death of Stalin, as the accompanying article from a 1954 issue of *Look* indicates.) But at least the film ended with the bucolic vision of the Gouzenkos walking along a sunny country road as two dour government bodyguards follow behind, lugging the family's picnic basket.

The first of the postwar "Imagine if . . ." dramatizations of the Russians conquering and enslaving America, *Is This Tomorrow*, was published in 1947 by the Catechetical Guild Educational Society of St. Paul, Minnesota. At ten cents a copy, this fifty-two-page, full-color comic book was a smashing success. It enjoyed several reprintings, and was used as a giveaway, presumably distributed to church groups. Ultimately, some four million copies were printed, which would suggest a readership in the neighborhood of ten or twelve million, factoring in the normal pass-along life of a comic book. Despite the success of *Is This Tomorrow*, the Guild withheld national distribution of its next two exercises in Red-hot hysteria, *Blood Is the Harvest* and *If the Devil Would Talk*, both of which were prepared in 1950 but killed in committee, perhaps for being redundant.

Feverish Commie-takeover scenarios would emerge in the mass media in the years to come, including *Life* magazine's "The Reds Have a Standard Plan for Taking Over a New Country" (1948), the M-G-M cartoon "Make Mine Freedom" (1948), Columbia Pictures' 1952 film *Invasion U.S.A.*, the 1962 television special *Red Nightmare* ("Presented by the Department of Defense"), and such comic book extravaganzas as "The Sneak Attack" in the first issue of *Atomic War* (1952). But none of them could quite match *Is This Tomorrow* for pure holy terror.

Look
VOLUME 12, NUMBER 16
AUGUST 3, 1948

Killers could strike during darkness to spread con- shows. It's one of the dramatic scenes LOOK enacted
fusion throughout a terror-gripped city, as this picture for its picture story beginning on page 24.

If you're going to take over America, you have to start *some*where.
According to "Could the Reds Seize Detroit?", *Look* magazine's 1948 docudrama, "Many factors
make Detroit a focal point of Communist activity. Not the least of these is its geographical
location. Only a narrow river separates the city from Canada, a foreign country. Ignoring the
formalities of legal entrance, Red agents can shuttle back and forth, as rum-runners did during
Prohibition days." The piece goes on to note that while the three-to-six-thousand "sinister"
Communists believed to inhabit Detroit may seem like modest numbers for implementing a
takeover, their ranks would quickly be augmented by the prisoners of the Wayne County Jail,
who would be freed, recruited, and armed within minutes of the "blitzkrieg-style" attack. And
then, "for at least one night, Detroit could know the chaos and horror that Bogotá, Colombia
knew this spring when a Red-inspired revolt unleashed a reign of terror and destruction."

Reds would find these top men of Detroit Police Department tough foes

Superintendent Morgan.   Senior Inspector Furlong.   Senior Inspector Wysocki.   Senior Inspector Throop.

Dramatized with the cooperation of formidable Detroit police commissioner Harry Toy and his legion of 4,000 officers, along with the help of the Wayne County Road Patrol and Detroit mayor Eugene I. Van Antwerp, "Could the Reds Seize Detroit?" is a paean to paramilitary passion and paranoia.

Stabbing, holdup would give
Reds control of police radio
(Continued on next page)

MOST TALKED ABOUT **DRAMA** OF OUR TIME!

The **RED MENACE**

A REPUBLIC PICTURE

"SEE . . . How a Psychopathic Love-starved Woman Defies the Law!"

"SEE . . . How a Man Is Driven to Suicide Rather Than Bend to the Yoke of Tyranny!"

"SEE . . . How a Man Is Brutally Murdered Because He Challenges Gangster Rule!"

That ad from Republic Pictures' marvelously sensationalistic campaign neatly conveys the flavor of its 1949 film *The Red Menace*, the studio's overheated exposé of Communist Party treachery. Narrated by Los Angeles city councilman Lloyd G. Douglas, *The Red Menace* stands as the only movie ever made in which every line of dialogue is a speech. The plot: When angry vet Bill Jones finds the folks at Veteran's Aid unresponsive to his complaints, he is targeted by Red agents as a disillusioned sap ripe for recruitment into the Party. Seduced by B-girl Molly, a very poor man's Mata Hari (see photo), the easily manipulated lug starts attending adult education courses in Communist thought. There he falls for his attractive teacher, Nina Petrovka, who dispenses the Party line even as she becomes increasingly aware that her cell is run by a collection of thugs and lunatics. When a sensitive Jewish poet named Solomon is driven to commit suicide after the Party has excommunicated him for heresy--he wrote a poem about Marx that credited Hegel (what rhymes with Hegel?)--Bill and Nina flee. Even Molly, the lapsed Catholic, will return to the Church and the arms of her forgiving mother, as the local padre beams. No wonder the Communist paper the *Daily People's World* called the film "stupid but dangerous."

A valentine to the packs of HUAC investigators nipping at Hollywood's heels, *The Red Menace* won a commendation for Republic studio boss Herbert J. Yates. If *Patton* was Nixon's favorite film, *The Red Menace* was probably J. Edgar Hoover's. The "world-wide Marxist racket," as one character refers to Communism, never seemed so pathetically inept.

HER BEAUTY served a
mob of terror whose one
mission is to destroy!

I MARRIED a Communist

starring

LARAINE DAY · ROBERT RYAN · JOHN AGAR

with THOMAS GOMEZ · JANIS CARTER

Executive Producer SID ROGELL

Produced by JACK J. GROSS · Directed by ROBERT STEVENSON
Screen Play by CHARLES GRAYSON and ROBERT HARDY ANDREWS

Inspired in part by the case of Harry Bridges (the leader of the West Coast Longshoremen whom the government spent some thirteen years and millions of dollars trying to convict of allowing Reds to infiltrate his union) the RKO film *I Married a Communist* opened in New York in the Fall of 1949, just as Bridges' final trial (after endless appeals) and the Foley Square trial of eleven CPA leaders were being conducted. But the fortuitous publicity tie-ins must not have helped, because RKO studio boss Howard Hughes had the film yanked before it went into national distribution. He rereleased it months later under the less polarizing title *The Woman on Pier 13*, to no avail. Audiences still didn't want to see this unremitting grim tale of dumb Americans unable to cope with the pitiless Communists and their insidious plan to take over the waterfront. (Today the shipping industry; tomorrow the world!) By the time one poor dupe (actor John Agar) has been run over by a car, a Commie seductress (Janis Carter) has been pushed out a window for going soft on the Party, and our "hero" Brad (Robert Ryan) has been shot to death in a warehouse donnybrook with the Red cell leader Nixon (Thomas Gomez), paying customers were probably running for the exits in droves (straight to the local FBI office). Still, the film had its moments. This excerpt from the screenplay shows Nixon blackmailing Brad with his past history (as Party member "Frank Johnson") to force him to turn over control of the longshoremen's union to the Reds:

Photofest

NIXON: All right, Johnson.

   (Brad advances to him grimly.)

BRAD: I came down here to get something settled...

NIXON: (interrupts) I sent for you--Johnson--because I wanted to refresh your memory about what can happen to Party members who betray their Party oath. In your case, you're going to be given the opportunity to redeem yourself . . .

BRAD: Look--I'm out of the Party. I've been out for years. You've got nothing I want . . . What do you want from me?

   (As he speaks, Nixon dons spectacles--writes on slip of paper. Brad's half-plea, half-challenge means nothing.)

NIXON: (interrupting again) Beginning immediately, two-fifths of your salary will be deposited in this bank, to the account of this organization. (hands slip across table) The organization is listed as a charity. Therefore, your contributions are tax-deductible. That's very important to some of our higher-bracket members. Incidentally, Johnson, we know the exact amount of your income from all sources.

BRAD: I bet you do! Just like the good old days.

NIXON: Not quite. Frank Johnson could make speeches at meetings--pass out handbills--brawl in the streets. Mr. Bradley Collins can't. Your present position qualifies you for much more important service to the Party.

BRAD: Now, look . . .

NIXON: (interrupts) You'll be notified when I have orders for you. That's all.

THEY SAID IT!

When Angela Calomiris completed her seven years of posing as a Communist for the FBI's Subversive Squad in 1949, she was asked to testify as to the reading habits of Party members before Judge Medina in New York's Foley Square, where eleven of the nation's top Communists were on trial for advocating the overthrow of the U.S. government. Calomiris identified and commented upon a variety of Communist works that had been entered as evidence. Unlike her fellow infilitrators, Matt ("I Posed as a Communist for the F.B.I.") Cvetic and Herb (*I Led Three Lives*) Philbrick, both of whom also testified for the government, Angela Calomiris was not able to parlay this moment in the spotlight into a full-time career as an American watchdog against Communism. But in 1950 Lippincott *did* publish her story as *Red Masquerade: Undercover for the F.B.I.*, the Appendix of which provides us with the following excerpts from Marx, Lenin, Stalin et al. that she read into the trial record. Since the eleven Reds were found guilty and sent to prison, it may be said that Ms. Calomiris left her own mark on history, even if her heroism wasn't immortalized on film, radio, and/or television.

"The Communists disdain to conceal their views and aims. They openly declare that their ends can be attained only by the forcible overthrow of all existing social conditions. Let the ruling classes tremble at a Communist revolution. The proletarians have nothing to lose but their chains. They have a world to win.

"Workingmen of all countries, unite!"

--Karl Marx and Friedrich Engels, *Manifesto of the Communist Party* (1848)

"The actual strength of the Communist movement in the United States is not something that can be accurately stated in just so many figures . . . . The influence of the Party stretches far and wide beyond the limits of its actual membership.

"The American revolution, when the workers have finally seized power, will develop even more swiftly in all its phases than has the Russian revolution. This is because in the United States objective conditions are more ripe for revolution than they were in old Russia."

--William Z. Foster,
Toward Soviet America (1932)

"The liberation of the oppressed class is impossible not only without a violent revolution, but also without the destruction of the apparatus of state power, which was created by the ruling class. In order to win the majority of the population to its side, the proletariat must first of all overthrow the bourgeoisie and seize state power and, secondly, it must introduce Soviet rule, smash to pieces the old state apparatus, and thus at one blow undermine the rule, authority and influence of the bourgeois and of the petty-bourgeois compromisers in the ranks of the non-proletarian toiling masses. Thirdly, the proletariat must completely and finally destroy the influence of the bourgeoisie and of the petty-bourgeoisie compromisers among the majority of the non-proletarian toiling masses by the revolutionary satisfaction of their economic needs at the expense of the exploiters."

--Lenin,
State and Revolution (1917)

"The dictatorship of the proletariat is a revolutionary power based on the use of force against the bourgeoisie. The seizure of power is only the beginning. For many reasons the bourgeoisie that is overthrown in one country remains for a long time stronger than the proletariat which has overthrown it. Therefore, the whole point is to retain power, to consolidate it, to make it invincible."
 --Joseph Stalin,
  Foundations of Leninism (1939)

"The Role and Aim of the Communist Party: As the leader and organizer of the proletariat, the Communist Party of the U.S.A. leads the working class in the fight for the revolutionary overthrow of capitalism, for the establishment of a Socialist Soviet Republic of the United States, for the complete abolition of classes, for the establishment of socialism, the first stage of the classless Communist society."
 --J. Peters,
 The Communist Party Manual (1935)

WHAT IS A COMMUNIST?

WHITTAKER CHAMBERS

One of the strangest figures to emerge from the hysteria of the Cold War, ex-Communist Whittaker Chambers became a household name when he not only named former State Department official Alger Hiss as a Communist before HUAC in an August 1948 session but repeated the charge on *Meet the Press* ten days later. That provoked Hiss into filing a $50,000 slander suit against Chambers--and thus the battle was joined.

ALGER HISS

Originally, Chambers claimed that Hiss was part of a Washington, D.C., Communist cell in the 1930s and that he and his cohorts were attempting to infiltrate the U.S. government. Once Hiss sued him, however, Chambers contradicted his earlier testimony and upgraded Hiss's affronts to engaging in espionage. The evidence: sixty-nine documents that Hiss had supposedly given to Chambers for use by the Party and which Chambers had suddenly rediscovered after setting them atop an unused dumbwaiter back in 1938. Four of the documents had been handwritten by Hiss, which he admitted upon seeing them; the other sixty-five were typed summaries of trade agreements, which Hiss hadn't seen and which didn't originate in his department.

And then came the revelation that guaranteed the case a permanent spot in the Red Menace Hall of Fame: Chambers called ambitious young Congressman Dick Nixon and told him that he'd withheld five rolls of microfilm that had been hidden in a pumpkin on his farm. When the grand jury considered the damning microfilm--the only two rolls developed contained various State Department documents, some in code--they indicted Hiss on two counts of perjury, rather than the more serious charge of espionage. A month later, Chambers recanted on his ability to place Hiss in the Washington cell, and the first trial ended with a hung jury. But Hiss was retried in November of 1949, and this time he was convicted on the two counts of perjury and sentenced to five years in prison.

As Curt Gentry's account of the arrest and trials in *J. Edgar Hoover: The Man and the Secrets* makes clear, the Hiss case was one of the greatest bag jobs of all time, even by the rock-bottom standards Hoover had set for spy trials. When Hiss was permitted to examine the three undeveloped rolls of microfilm in 1975 under the Freedom of Information Act, he found that the damning evidence that had helped convict him--without the contents ever being revealed (for "security" reasons)--comprised the following: two rolls of film from the U.S. Navy that contained instructions on how to use life rafts and fire extinguishers, and a third roll that was blank. As for Chambers, his self-serving 1951 autobiography, *Witness*, became a bestseller and a Book-of-the-Month Club selection.

"J. EDGAR HOOVER: COMMUNIST HUNTER NO. 1"

FBI Probes Blast Ship's Cargo

LYNCH CAPTIVE GIVES UP TO FBI

Escaped Mob, Hid With Friends

FBI Nabs Youth Here In Michigan Slaying

FBI SEIZES 6 AS SPIES, TWO INSTATEDEPT.

FBI Seizes 2 as Bosses of 5-State Auto-Theft Ring

FBI'S HIDDEN STRUGGLE AGAINST SPIES CONTINUES

Trial of Enemy Agents at Governors Island Reveals Enemy Activity

MAJOR CRIME WAVE DUE, SAYS HOOVER

Probe of KKK By FBI Seen

FBI HEAD BRANDS COMMUNIST PARTY A 'FIFTH COLUMN'

WIDER AID TO YOUTH URGED BY HOOVER

"**N**inety-six point nine percent of all arrests made by the bureau in 1945 resulted in convictions." If they were all conducted at the level of the Alger Hiss case of 1948 and prosecuted with evidence of the quality provided by undercover operatives like Matthew (*I Was a Communist for the F.B.I.*) Cvetic and Herbert (*I Led Three Lives*) Philbrick, the only question is: How on earth did the FBI lose the other 3.1 percent of the cases? "J. Edgar Hoover: Communist Hunter No. 1," from a 1947 issue of *Look*, was typical of the respectful (not to say fearful) treatment Hoover received from the media during his lifetime, even though he was detested by FDR, Truman, and most of the other Presidents whose terms of office he outlasted. For a less respectful account of the loathsome FBI Director's accomplishments, see Curt Gentry's damning *J. Edgar Hoover: The Man and the Secrets* (Norton, 1991).

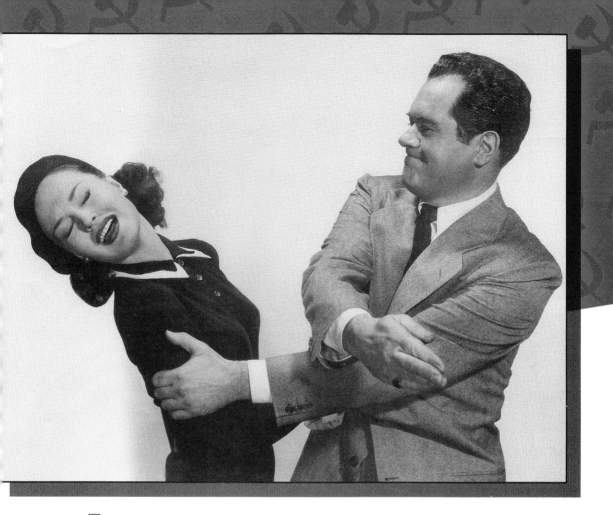

All the world may be a stage, but for Matt Cvetic and Herb Philbrick, real-life volunteer undercover agents for Hoover's FBI throughout most of the forties, the courtroom was the venue that catapulted them into the glamorous world of show biz. Cvetic had infiltrated the Communist Party in Pittsburgh, while Philbrick had used his uncanny intelligence to penetrate the Red cells of Boston. When the two of them testified independently in 1949, helping to convict several top Party members of conspiracy to overthrow the U.S. government, their fortunes were as good as made.

Cvetic, a hard-drinking lout who reportedly once thrashed his sister-in-law badly enough to hospitalize her, sold his first-person account to *The Saturday Evening Post*, which serialized his heroics as "I Posed as a Communist for the FBI" (written with the help of Pete Martin). A radio series followed. Then, in 1951, Warner Brothers released the film version, with Frank Lovejoy portraying the man who (it is suggested) singlehandedly brought the Communist Party to its knees. Pittsburgh celebrated the film's April premiere with a "Matthew Cvetic Day," complete with parade. Incredibly, *I Was a Communist for the F.B.I.* was nominated for an Academy Award as the best *documentary* of the year.

"I LED THREE LIVES"

Not to be outdone, Herb Philbrick sold McGraw-Hill his account of how he toppled the Boston branch of the Party, which was published as *I Led Three Lives* in 1952. A year later, the nationally syndicated television series was unleashed on America, featuring episodes with such titles as "Communist Extortion Racket," "Parcels for Poland," "Secret Printing Press," "Party Discipline," and so on. (Here Philbrick is shown at the knee of his TV alter ego, actor Richard Carlson, who soon would demonstrate keener judgment by accepting the lead in *Creature from the Black Lagoon*.) Small wonder that Philbrick was awarded his own spot at the New York *Herald Tribune* as a "Red Underground" columnist.

Thus America rewards its loyal servants. Between them, Cvetic and Philbrick named over five hundred Communist agents, quite a few of whom turned out to be other undercover FBI agents. If only Cvetic and Philbrick had teamed up their fervid imaginations, we might now remember them as one of the era's great comedy teams, Red-smashing rivals to Abbott and Costello and Martin and Lewis.

"Spying on America is Easy"

Sure it is--if you happen to own a pumpkin patch.

"Spying on America Is Easy," from the September 1950 issue of *Hit!* magazine, makes reference to Judith Coplon, one of the few actual Communist spies the FBI ever managed to arrest and convict. Unfortunately--and typically, for the FBI--the conviction didn't stick.

Coplon was a Justice Department employee who worked in the Foreign Agents Registration Section. For years she had been passing classified documents to one Valentin Gubitchev, a member of the UN Secretariat. Although Hoover had Coplon pegged as a KGB spy late in 1948, he was determined to catch her in the act, rather than merely dismiss her from government service. And so an elaborate sting operation was put into effect, with a 115-page phony espionage report as the bait. It worked; Coplon was caught Red-handed passing a copy of the report to Gubitchev (who also happened to be her lover), and was arrested on March 4, 1949. She was a dead duck.

The jury at her first trial found her guilty of espionage and sentenced her to ten years in prison. Coplon was then tried on a charge of conspiracy to transmit documents to a foreign power, this time with Gubitchev as her codefendant. Although this second trial produced the disturbing information that Coplon and Gubitchev had been arrested without warrants, and that illegal wiretaps had been conducted before, during, and after their arrest, they were convicted on March 7, 1950, and given fifteen-year jail terms. At the request of the State Department, Gubitchev was deported, proof positive that our fears about the UN offering a haven to "foes of the American way of life" (as the accompanying article puts it) were not groundless.

But Coplon never had to serve her sentence. Judge Learned Hand of the U.S. Circuit Court of Appeals heard her appeal in December and ruled that both of her convictions had been based on tainted information and procedure. Coplon was free--almost. An enraged and embarrassed Hoover kept her under indictment for the next seventeen years, making her a captive of New York City.

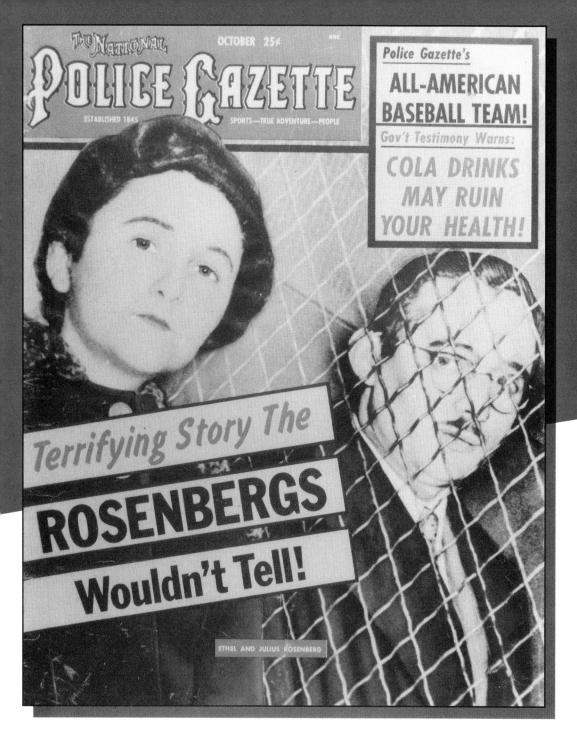

The National

POLICE GAZETTE

OCTOBER 25¢

ESTABLISHED 1845 · SPORTS—TRUE ADVENTURE—PEOPLE

Police Gazette's
ALL-AMERICAN BASEBALL TEAM!

Gov't Testimony Warns:
COLA DRINKS MAY RUIN YOUR HEALTH!

Terrifying Story The
ROSENBERGS
Wouldn't Tell!

ETHEL AND JULIUS ROSENBERG

The espionage question was less easily resolved in the case of Julius and Ethel Rosenberg, the husband-wife "team" accused of masterminding an atomic spy ring in 1950. Ethel's dimwitted brother, David Greenglass, had been arrested for pocketing (literally!) a lump of uranium from Los Alamos and stealing atomic secrets, and was put in a jail cell with self-styled Kremlin agent Harry Gold. Greenglass named Julius as his master spy, and later threw in Ethel for good measure. The Rosenbergs were picked up by the FBI on the basis of such evidence as a torn jello box top, and put behind bars at Sing Sing for three years, during which time they were blamed for everything from the outbreak of the Korean War to measles and mumps. Finally, on June 19, 1953, they were sent to the electric chair--first Julius, then Ethel ---without ever having divulged the names of their cohorts in espionage.

Were there any? To this date, history has not produced a single one. But President Eisenhower was certainly not indulging any second thoughts about the extent of the Rosenbergs' guilt that day in June. After refusing for a second time to issue an order of Executive clemency, Ike offered this chilly comment: "I can only say that, by immeasurably increasing the chances of atomic war, the Rosenbergs may have condemned to death tens of millions of innocent people all over the world."

While the execution of the Rosenbergs was greeted with outrage by much of America, there was at least *one* beacon of integrity that courageously backed Ike. The *Police Gazette* rushed its October 1953 issue to press with the cover story you see here: "Terrifying Story the ROSENBERGS Wouldn't Tell!" As penned by George McGrath, this vitriolic essay posited that "there are an estimated 160 Communist agents in the U.S. and Canada who are plotting to destroy us." Enumerating the Rosenbergs' crimes with growing relish, McGrath went on to note that they

> planted and cultivated the poison of Communist treachery in the minds of scores of impressionable American youths who, if left alone, would have grown up to be patriotic citizens . . . Ethel and Julius Rosenberg will go down in infamy as traitors to the United States. The Rosenbergs did not have to die. They could have cheated the electric chair by exposing the sinister Soviet spy ring operating throughout America. But they refused to talk--and by their silence, they continue to betray their country in death as they did in life.

So they went to their deaths "in silence"--if you can call pleading your innocence for three years silence. Perhaps if the Rosenbergs had had a "sinister Soviet spy ring" to expose, the *Police Gazette* would have smiled on them *in memoriam*.

Though best known for its fine annual series of baseball cards, the Philadelphia-based Bowman Gum Company's crowning achievement was its 1951 set, "Children's Crusade Against Communism." An inspired mixture of *our* All-Star, four-star generals, *their* Murderers' Row (hottest rookie card: #57, Ho Chi Minh!), and scenes of mayhem ranging from actual battles in Korea to fanciful renderings of life after the Bomb, these cards took kiddie kulture to places it had never been before. It was a toss-up whether the illustration on the front or the invective on the back was more fun. All this, and a stick of petrified bubble-gum, too! Just one small complaint: the Stalin card (#71) neglected to list his lifetime stats.

CHILDREN'S CRUSADE AGAINST COMMUNISM

35. Visit by Red Police

Why is this Russian family being arrested? Perhaps the radio is a clue. These people may have been listening to the "Voice of America." The "Voice," you know, is a radio program in which our State Department tells the truth about the free world. The Red leaders do not want the Russian people to learn what real freedom is like. They might ask it for themselves. But who reported that this family tuned in on the "Voice"? Perhaps someone they thought was a friend. Who can tell who may be a spy for the secret police?

 FIGHT THE RED MENACE

© 1951 Bowman Gum, Inc., Phila., Pa., U.S.A.

The original Children's Crusade, incidentally, took place in 1212, when fifty thousand children followed Stephen of Vendôme and Nicholas of Cologne south in an attempt to cross the Mediterranean to the Holy Land. Some were seized in Marseilles, others were seized and sold into slavery when they arrived in Egypt. On balance, trading bubble-gum cards seems the better way to go.

A NICE RED APPLE FROM THE TEACHER

When Mao Tse-tung finally defeated the nationalist forces of Chiang Kai-shek in the fall of 1949, it was hard to tell who was unhappier over the news, the U.S. or the U.S.S.R. On the surface, the victory of the Communists in China should have pleased Stalin, the acknowledged head of the world Communist movement. But Mao's triumph embarrassed Stalin. He had predicted that Chiang's nationalist forces were not yet ripe for the conquering, and tried to rein in Mao. Worse, he had consistently favored other Chinese Communist leaders over Mao. But in the end he *had* to acknowledge Mao, and so it was Mao who attended Stalin's seventieth birthday party in Moscow in December of 1949.

But Mao had not traveled all that way just to help cut the cake. In February of 1950, he and Stalin signed a treaty of alliance between the two nations that guaranteed Red China both economic aid and access to an armada of Soviet technicians. Those Stalin granted, however grudgingly. But Mao's request for the atom bomb was brusquely denied. For his part, Stalin extracted from the Sino-Soviet Friendship Treaty the use of bases and rail lines throughout mainland China. He also proved himself a sport by turning over to Mao the top Soviet agent within the Chinese Politburo, who, naturally, was shot in short order.

No sooner had the unwelcome Mao finished his business in Moscow than Ho Chi Minh appeared. As reported in Robert Conquest's *Stalin: Breaker of Nations*, on this visit Ho was primarily interested in getting Stalin's autograph; the trophy was later lifted from Ho's luggage by the secret police. (The old Bolshevik had been a senior Comintern agent back in the twenties, and was probably just yanking surly Joe's chain.)

Then, in March, Kim Il Sung arrived from North Korea asking for official Party approval of his plan to attack the South. Stalin--who must have been low on hors d'oeuvres by this point -- gave his blessing. On June 25, South Korea was invaded, and the Cold War suddenly became Red-hot.

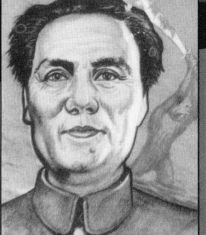

CHILDREN'S CRUSADE AGAINST COMMUNISM

2. MacArthur Heads UN Forces

North Korean Reds attacked South Korea in what is believed to be part of a communist plan gradually to conquer the whole world. The United Nations pitched in to help the South Koreans, like your dad would help the folks next door if some bad men were beating them up. The troops sent to Korea for the UN were put under command of General Douglas MacArthur. "Mac" has a long military record. But you know him best as the general who led the Allied forces to victory in the Pacific during the second world war.

 FIGHT THE RED MENACE

CHILDREN'S CRUSADE AGAINST COMMUNISM

47. War-Maker

Mao Tse-tung is the leader of the Chinese Reds who attacked the United Nations forces in Korea. His army was built up, in the first place, with the help of outlaws. Later the Russian Reds supplied him with arms and advisers. He captured the China mainland in three years of savage warfare against the Nationalist government. Mao delights in war. History, he says, "is written in blood and iron." The free world must find a way to keep war-makers like Mao Tse-tung from shedding the blood of innocent people.

 FIGHT THE RED MENACE

A footnote to the success of Mao's forces in China is the story of O. Edmund Clubb, our Consul General in Peking when it was seized in 1949. Clubb became our last diplomat stationed on mainland China, and thus it fell to him to haul down the American flag before he left in April 1950. It was a symbolic act for which he would pay dearly. Reassigned as chief of the China desk at the State Department upon his return to the U.S., Clubb was suspended in 1951 as a security risk. A loyalty board had discovered a report Clubb submitted in 1932 acknowledging the popularity of the Communists with many of the Chinese, and stating that the Chinese Nationalist government, which the U.S. was supporting, was particularly corrupt. (Sound familiar?) Although Clubb was cleared on appeal, he resigned five days after being reassigned to an obscure job in the State Department. Years later, "the man who had lost China" would write in his memoir, "the Government of which I had long been a part had been disloyal to me."

For the simplest possible explanation of the roots of the Korean conflict, we again direct our attention to the "Children's Crusade Against Communism" bubble-gum card series of 1951, which offers all the information necessary on its Mao and General MacArthur card entries. (By the time the Korean War ended, in 1953, one of those estimable gentlemen would no longer be employed. Hint: he wasn't Chinese.)

BOMB
SHELTERS

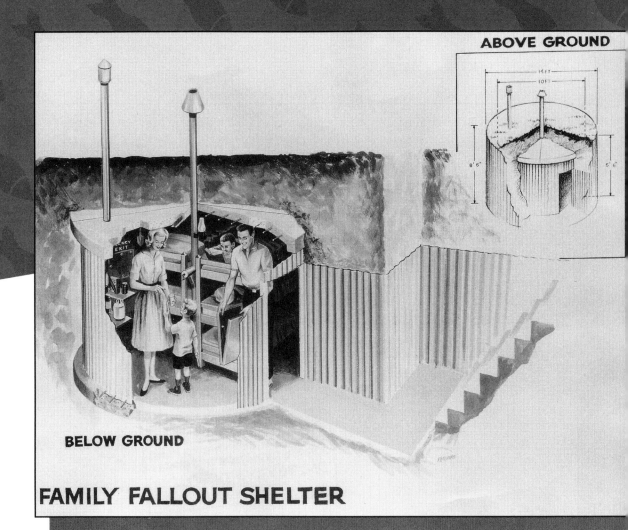

ABOVE GROUND

BELOW GROUND

FAMILY FALLOUT SHELTER

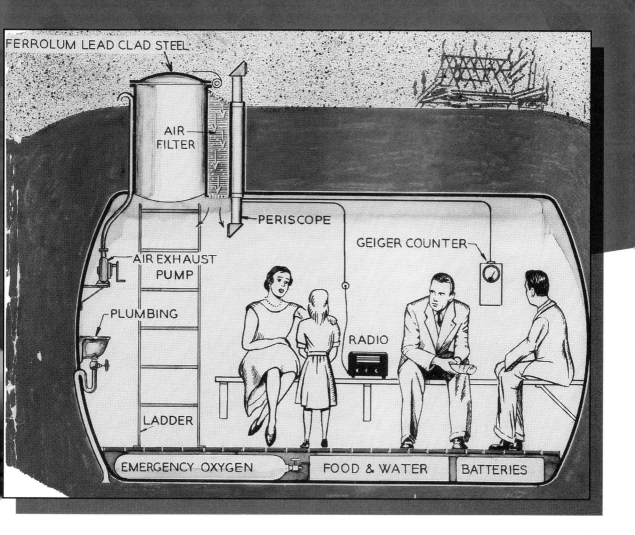

FERROLUM LEAD CLAD STEEL

AIR FILTER

PERISCOPE

GEIGER COUNTER

AIR EXHAUST PUMP

PLUMBING

RADIO

LADDER

EMERGENCY OXYGEN   FOOD & WATER   BATTERIES

Once Russia detonated its first atomic bomb, on August 29, 1949, it was only a matter of weeks before the first "civil defense" plans and products began to surface. The family situated in the "Family Fallout Shelter" seems to be having a much better time than their counterparts stuck in the "Family Size Atomic Safety Shelter"--possibly because Mom remembered to pack some snacks in the first case, while Dad forgot the bunk beds in the latter. Who wants to wait out months or years of radioactive fallout while sitting on a bench?

Mickey Spillane

ONE LONELY NIGHT

The Sensational New Mystery
by the author of "I, The Jury"

A SIGNET BOOK
Complete and Unabridged

N·A·L
SIGNET
BOOKS   *...Good Reading for the Millions*

MICKEY SPILLANE—
TODAY'S FASTEST SELLING MYSTERY WRITER!
whose stories have sold 25,000,000 copies in Signet
editions alone!

MIKE HAMMER—
THE MOST FAMOUS PRIVATE EYE IN THE BUSINESS
swears to avenge a gorgeous red-headed streetwalker
and battles his way along a bloody, bullet-strewn path
from a millionaire's mansion through glittering night-
spots and seductively lit apartments in this scorching
murder mystery about the white slave racket.

Published by the New American Library

"**C**hampion of the Tough Mystery Writers"--so
his paperback publisher knighted Mickey Spillane
in the fifties, after his five Mike Hammer novels
had sold upwards of thirty million copies. *One
Lonely Night* was fourth in the series, and it
contained all the standard elements of Spillane's
work to date--treacherous females, frightful
villains, and an incorruptible (if slightly dim) hero--
with one key innovation: this time, private eye
Mike Hammer is facing off against a horde of
Communist thugs, whose plan is (Ho hum . . .) a
takeover of the United States.

A Commie. She was a jerky Red. She owned all the trimmings and she was still a Red. What the hell was she hoping for, a government order to share it all with the masses? Yeah. A joint like this would suddenly assume a new owner under a new regime. A fat little general, a ranking secret policeman, somebody. Sure, it's great to be a Commie...as long as you're top dog. Who the hell was supposed to be fooled by all the crap?

Gladow spoke. The aides spoke. Then the general spoke. He pulled his tux jacket down when he rose and glared at the audience. I had to sit there and listen to it. It was propaganda right off the latest Moscow cable and it turned me inside out. I wanted to feel the butt of an M-1 against my shoulder pointing at those bastards up there on the rostrum and feel the pleasant impact as it spit slugs into their guts.

Sure, you can sit down at night and read about the hogwash they hand out. Maybe you're fairly intelligent and can laugh at it. Believe me, it isn't funny. They use the very thing we build up, our own government and our own laws, to undermine the things we want.

It wasn't a very complicated speech the general made. It was plain, bitter poison and they cheered him noiselessly. He was making plain one thing. There were still too many people who didn't go for Communism and not enough who did and he gave a plan of organization that had worked in a dozen countries already. One armed Communist was worth twenty capitalists without guns. It was Hitler all over again. A powerful Communist government already formed would be there to take over when the big upset came, and according to him it was coming soon.

Read the papers today. See what it says about the Red Menace. See how they play up their sneaking, conniving ways. They're supposed to be clever, bright as hell. They were dumb as horse manure as far as I was concerned. They were a pack of thugs thinking they could outsmart a world. Great. That coffee-urn trick was just great.

Although *One Lonely Night* was never filmed, the next Mike Hammer adventure, *Kiss Me, Deadly*, was transformed into one of the best Cold War movies in 1955 by director Robert Aldrich, who replaced the Mafia goons of the book with Reds who have stolen an atomic device.

The above excerpts from *One Lonely Night* convey Spillane's inimitable frenzied rhetoric, which, more than any other element of his work, always captured and delighted the hearts of his xenophobic audience.

Archive Photos

THE WHIP HAND

FOREIGN DEATH PLOT PERILS NATION'S GREATEST CITIES!

The startling, shocking, amazing story of secret enemy madmen of science *within our borders* ... and their fiendish germ-death plot to destroy every U.S. human!

CARLA BALENDA
ELLIOTT REID

See
AND THRILL TO:

- Foreign terror-scientists planning mass murder!
- "Death laboratory" hidden in our own Northwoods!
- Lethal germs bred to infect water and milk supplies!
- Human guinea-pigs for cruel death-germ "doctors"!

Production Designed and Directed by WILLIAM CAMERON MENZIES
Screenplay by GEORGE BRICKER and FRANK L. MOSS

As the fifties began, Hollywood swung into high gear to

demonstrate the height of its patriotism. Each studio had to have at least one maniacally pure melodrama it could cart out when--not *if*--HUAC came sniffing at its door. Powerful Warner Brothers, feeling vulnerable for having made the pro-Stalin *Mission to Moscow* in 1943 (of which HUAC was happy to remind them), made doubly certain it had cleansed itself by releasing *I Was a Communist for the F.B.I.* in 1951, and *Big Jim McClain* in 1952, one of John Wayne's most rabidly patriotic films (in a career chock full of them).

Mighty M-G-M, embarrassed at having produced that wartime love letter to the Russian people, *Song of Russia* (1943), atoned by conjuring up *The Red Danube*, with Janet Leigh as a ballerina pursued by Russian agents, and *Conspirator*, with Elizabeth Taylor as a young bride who comes to realize that hubby Robert Taylor is a Commie spy (both 1949). Columbia Pictures offered a pair of deuces in 1952: *Walk East on Beacon*, with the FBI hunting spies in Boston, and *Invasion U.S.A.*, which dramatized a Red takeover of the United States (though it all turned out to have been the shared hallucination of several patrons sitting together at a bar). Having chickened out on *I Married a Communist* by retitling it a few months later, RKO tried again with *The Whip Hand*, a 1951 "B" release that posited a reporter stumbling upon a Commie germ-warfare plant somewhere in the north woods. This tall tale, despite offering Raymond Burr as a Red thug, was no *Citizen Kane*.

LEO McCAREY'S **MY SON JOHN**

starring

HELEN HAYES
VAN HEFLIN
ROBERT WALKER
DEAN JAGGER

Screenplay by
Myles Connolly and Leo McCarey
Adaptation by John Lee Mahin
Produced and Directed by Leo McCarey
A Paramount Picture

But the honor roll was topped by Paramount Pictures' 1952 exercise in advanced dementia, *My Son, John*. Director Leo McCarey had already been certified by HUAC as a friendly witness after his testimony before them in 1947, but he further distinguished himself in 1950 by heading a movement, together with Cecil B. DeMille, to have all members of the Screen Directors Guild sign a loyalty oath. *My Son, John*, then, wasn't merely a movie: it *was* a loyalty oath. Helen Hayes and Dean Jagger portray parents who have growing suspicions that their son John, memorably presented by Robert Walker, is a godless Communist. Even as his brothers are laying their lives on the line in Korea, Walker sneers at his American Legionnaire father, a dim bulb of a dad if ever there was one, and condescends to his addlepated, glove-chewing, hyperkinetic mom.

Photofest

(Helen Hayes hadn't seen work in Hollywood for seventeen years prior to this film, and her performance here must have cinched the next seventeen, as well.)

Eventually, *My Son, John* becomes a struggle between the forces of atheism and the legions of Christ. Walker swears on a Holy Bible that he is not a Communist, yet Hayes cannot be deceived--she is, after all, a mother--and turns him over to the FBI, screaming, "He has to be punished!" Only then does Walker experience a change of heart (and soul). But on his way to confess his sins to the FBI, Walker is shot and killed by Commie agents. Which only goes to show how dumb those Reds were; they eliminated the turncoat Walker, but let his mom and pop remain at large to thump their Bibles and make furtive phone calls to the FBI. With them alive, the Party never had a chance.

"HOW WILL OUR LAWS AGAINST TRAITORS WORK?"

Communist Leader Foster and five of the defendants in the trial before Judge Medina: Stachel, Winston, Davis, Dennis and Williamson.

"The Internal Security Act of 1950, sometimes called the McCarran Act or the anticommunist law, is one of the most controversial and least understood laws in the history of the republic. Yet it is of high importance that Americans understand it, since it involves (1) our national safety and (2) individual liberties."

So began Beverly Smith's inquiry "How Will Our Laws Against Traitors Work?" which appeared in the January 13, 1951, issue of *The Saturday Evening Post*. The Internal Security Act--popularly named for Nevada's Senator Pat McCarran, an aging hack who, in fact, commandeered the legislation from an earlier version by congressmen Karl Mundt and (of all people) Richard Nixon--argued for the fingerprinting and registration of all "subversives" at large in the United States. As the *SEP* article reports, the act's passage by House and Senate was quite controversial. President Truman, who had himself imposed the Loyalty Order for federal government employees in 1947, immediately vetoed it, on the grounds that it "would make a mockery of our Bill of Rights [and] would actually weaken our internal security measures." But his veto was overridden by a humbling 89 percent majority vote, and McCarran's newly formed Senate Internal Security Subcommittee--working closely with Hoover's FBI--set up shop and conducted hearings for the next twenty-seven years. One of the more bucolic provisions of the McCarran Act was its authorization of concentration camps "for emergency situations."

The National **POLICE GAZETTE**
ESTABLISHED 1845   SPORTS—TRUE ADVENTURE—PEOPLE

MAY, 25¢

There's POLIO in Your Foods
Can SANDY SADDLER Beat the G. I. Jinx?

BIG ? of the DAY

Sen. McCARTHY

RIGHT OR WRONG?

(SEE PAGE 4)

SEN. JOSEPH McCARTHY

But the McCarran Act was only the tip of the inquisitorial iceberg. HUAC was still in operation, although it had been relatively quiet since its Hollywood Ten triumph, and it quickly had to spring back into action to prove its continuing validity. In 1951, HUAC began its second wave of show business hearings, far outstripping its 1947 predecessor in scope, fanfare, and shamelessness.

Needing a forum that would give full rein to his lust for the limelight, Senator Joseph McCarthy attached himself to the newly formed Senate Permanent Subcommittee on Investigations of the Senate Committee on Government Operations (trips off the tongue, doesn't it?), assuming its chairmanship in 1953. It was under the glare of that subcommittee's 1954 probe of the Army that Tail-gunner Joe would finally crash and burn.

Add to the above the "Red squads" that the police departments of cities such as New York, Los Angeles, Chicago, and Detroit all had established by this time, and it becomes clear that the number of actual Communist agents operating in the U.S. must have been infinitely less than the number of Feds, cops, and subcommittees bent on wiretapping, surveilling, exposing, interrogating, blackmailing, indicting, and imprisoning them. But then, as J. Edgar Hoover was fond of pointing out, "It only took twenty-three Commies to overthrow Russia."

By one estimate, some six thousand different romance comic books were published from the late forties through the fifties, the heyday of the genre. Understandably, the Red Menace was not one of the issues commonly dealt with in the pages of *Young Love*, *Sweethearts*, and *Confessions of the Lovelorn*. But every now and then, the Communist threat did somehow interfere with the love lives of the characters within these magazines, and the results were most instructive. Here are excerpts from the long-lost classics "Communist Kisses!" "Behind the Romantic Curtain," "Priority Kisses," and "I Was a Spy!", all published between 1951 and 1955. The anguished cry of a character in one of the stories--"I'm not going to let myself fall in love with a rotten Communist! I'm not! I swear it!"--expresses something we've all been through.

I WAS A
SLAVE IN SIBERIA

The prisoners were surrounded by barbed wire, watchtowers, machine-gun posts and blinding searchlights. One step out of line and the guards would shoot to kill—but a man will take desperate chances to be free.

By HENRYK ZABORSKI as told to SEYMOUR FREIDIN and WILLIAM RICHARDSON

"Aldona, shy and sad. I shall remember her always. We were not allowed to say good-by."

The man who lived this story and made the rough sketches that illustrate it may be the last to have escaped from Siberia while its inhuman prisons were under the rule of Lavrenti Beria. He was only 21 when he was captured and sent first to a prison where 2,000 women were herded together, then to a logging camp in the Siberian wilderness, from which he escaped and then bluffed his way on foot and by train across Russian Asia into Iran. Allied intelligence officers have verified the details of Henryk Zaborski's adventure from the time of his capture to his return to the land of the living.

Stalin's biggest public relations problem after the war was the world's growing awareness of his slave labor camps. The Russians had accumulated a vast reservoir of goodwill in the United States during the years when they fought with us against the Fascists, but it quickly drained when reports came out about the millions of men and women sentenced to hard labor in prison camps across the U.S.S.R. Although the camps had been around since the 1920s, their numbers began to swell after the purges of 1937-38, and by war's end they were too widespread to remain hidden. The publication by Yale University Press in 1947 of *Forced Labor in Soviet Russia*, by David J. Dallin and Boris I. Nicolaevsky, made official the state of affairs that Americans had been glad to ignore while Russia was our ally, and set off a wave of grim accounts of the sort shown here.

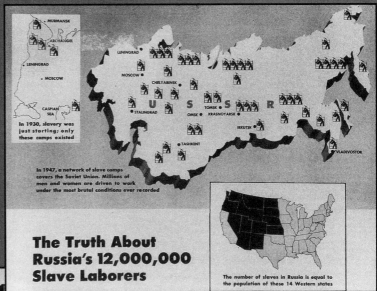

The Truth About
Russia's 12,000,000
Slave Laborers

The number of slaves in Russia is equal to
the population of these 14 Western states

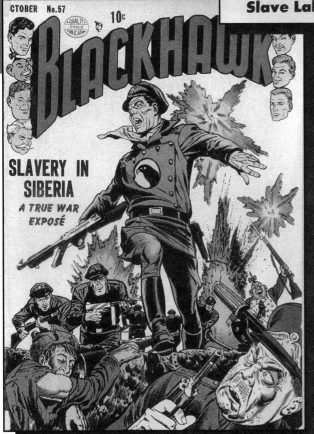

When Khrushchev emerged as the primary wielder of power after Stalin's death, he temporarily earned himself a quasi-humanitarian image by releasing large numbers of the interned. But once the Hungarian uprising of 1956 was so brutally crushed, we began to have second thoughts.

Here's Where Our Young Commies are Trained

By CRAIG THOMPSON

Do you imagine that all the youthful dupes of United States reds are embittered misfits from underprivileged families? Then this article, telling how and where American youngsters are taught contempt for their country, will enlighten you—and shock you.

IT takes more than a party card to transform the eager-beaver malcontents the Communist Party attracts into the tireless mischief-makers the party wants. Knowledge of how to manipulate twilight sleepers like Henry Wallace, when to attempt to wreck a man's business or what justifies treason does not come naturally—even to communists. These things have to be taught. To teach them, the communists have set up a chain of schools scattered across the United States.

The biggest school is in New York. It fills four floors of a gaunt yellow-brick building at 575 Avenue of the Americas, diagonally across the intersection of 16th Street from a Jesuit college, and it is called the Jefferson School of Social Science—"A People's University of Progressive Character."

The Jefferson School annually enrolls 3000 students—a fraction of the total signed up by the national chain, which stretches from Boston to the California Labor School in San Francisco, and includes establishments in Chicago, Philadelphia, Newark, Cleveland and other localities. Formerly some of these were identified by such names as the Abraham Lincoln, Walt Whitman or Samuel Adams schools, but after being listed as subversive by the United States Attorney General's office, they seem to have gone underground. All are part of what the communist Daily Worker describes as a "continuing process of recruiting and training new youthful forces for leadership within the Communist Party." Or, as one callow recruit phrased it: "The party will take anybody. You don't have to know anything to join—after you join they send you to school."

Alan Max, above, managing editor of the Daily Worker, gives course called Principles of Marxism.

It is as easy to enroll in the Jefferson School as to enter a neighborhood movie house. There are no scholastic requirements. The only questions asked are name, place of employment and trade-union affiliations. The fees are low—fifty cents to a dollar for individual forum lectures, and $7.50 for courses of ten. Special discounts are given to party groups and members of party affiliates such as the American Youth for Democracy. Once enrolled, the neophyte is plunged into a strange and, for some, exhilarating atmosphere of open conspiracy. Everyone speaks and acts on the assumption that everyone else is already a communist or about to become one. People who, elsewhere, will go to jail rather than admit being party members here openly proclaim it.

Recently, I sent a student into the Jefferson School. She was a young woman researcher who could take shorthand notes. She attended classes and talked to other students, setting down what she learned in a series of reports which run to thousands of words and are the substance of this article.

The hallmark of communist enterprises is squalor— a stage prop to induce more and bigger money gifts from its dupes—and the Jefferson School bears the approved stamp. Peeling paint hangs from its walls, the floors are bare and scuffed, the furniture nicked and rickety and the windows gray with grime. The student roster is by no means limited to doltish fledglings sent by the party cells. Although the school does lean heavily on the party machinery for its pupils, it also uses advertisements and articles in the party press and word-of-mouth promotion in legitimate universities, communist-front groups and

Commies are made, not born.

For the Communist Party of America, then, whose thirty thousand or so members were supposedly engaged in toppling the government of the United States, education must have been a clear and pressing need. At the height of the Red Scare, this translated into alarmist pieces like *Look* magazine's 1949 article, "Here's Where Our Young Commies Are Trained," and *The Saturday Evening Post*'s "Moscow's Mouthpiece in New York" (1953), both authored by the redoubtable Craig Thompson.

In describing the Jefferson School of Social Science, located at Sixth Avenue and Sixteenth Street in New York, Thompson contemptuously notes, "The hallmark of communist enterprises is squalor . . . and the Jefferson School bears the approved stamp. Peeling paint hangs from its walls, the floors are bared and scuffed, the furniture nicked and rickety and the windows gray with grime." (In other words, it looked like half of the publishing world in the New York of the 1990s.) In a spirit of fairness, Thompson admits that not all of the 3,000-member student body is comprised of "doltish fledglings."

The bible of U.S. Reds, the Daily Worker, has stayed in business 29 years despite a $5,000,000 deficit. Who finances this "newspaper"? Who owns it? What role does it play in the underground communist conspiracy? The inside story of

Moscow's Mouthpiece in New York

By CRAIG THOMPSON

Cigar-smoking John Gates, ex-editor of the Daily Worker, and John Williamson, party labor secretary, received five-year sentences for conspiring to overthrow the United States Government by force.

Thompson is just as scornful of the official newspaper of the Party, the *Daily Worker*, which, presumably, the young Commie dolts are able to read upon graduation. Established in 1924, the same year Stalin took power, the *Daily Worker* was located "on the eighth floor of a drab, nine-story loft building at 35 E. 12th Street in New York City, directly under the offices of the party's national committee." Thompson goes on to note that "the technique of creating a lie in order to brand all opponents of the Soviet Union and the Communist Party as liars or worse has been standard *Daily Worker* procedure."

If these two sorry organizations were at the vanguard of the Red takeover of the country, J. Edgar Hoover must have been sleeping quite soundly.

"IT'S LIKE A GERM. IT CAN SPREAD."

Appendix B

NATIONAL OPINION RESEARCH CENTER

and

AMERICAN INSTITUTE OF PUBLIC OPINION

8. Here is a list of topics which have been discussed in the papers recently. **(Hand respondent White Card)**

A. Which ones do you remember talking about with your friends in the last week or so?

A. Have talked about (12)		B. Most Important	C. Next Most Important
1	Atom or hydrogen bombs		
2	Communists in the United States		
3	Crime and juvenile delinquency		
4	Danger of World War III		
5	Farm prices		
6	High prices of things you buy		
7	High taxes		
8	Negro-white problems		
9	Possibility of another depression		
X	Threats to freedom in the United States		
Y	None of these, don't know		

9. In your opinion, how likely is it that World War III will break out **in the next two years?**

(15)

Very likely .... ☐ 1
Rather likely .... ☐ 2
Rather unlikely .... ☐ 3
Not likely at all .... ☐ 4
Don't know .... ☐ 0

10. **In the long run,** how likely is it that Communists can be stopped from taking over the rest of Europe without a World War?

(16)

Very likely .... ☐ 1
Rather likely .... ☐ 2
Rather unlikely .... ☐ 3
Not likely at all .... ☐ 4
Don't know .... ☐ 0

11. Suppose it turned out that the only way to stop the Communists from taking over the rest of Europe was for the United States to fight Russia. Should we let the Communists take over the rest of Europe or fight Russia?

(17)

Let Communists take over ...... ☐ 1
Fight Russia .... ☐ 2
Qualified (specify) .... ☐
Don't know .... ☐ 0

12. **In the long run,** how likely is it that Communists can be stopped from taking over the rest of Asia without a World War?

(18)

Very likely .... ☐ 1
Rather likely .... ☐ 2
Rather unlikely .... ☐ 3
Not likely at all .... ☐ 4
Don't know .... ☐ 0

13. Suppose it turned out that the only way to stop the Communists from taking over the rest of Asia was for the United States to fight Russia. Should we let the Communists take over the rest of Asia, or fight Russia?

(19)

Let Communists take over ...... ☐ 1
Fight Russia .... ☐ 2
Qualified (specify) .... ☐
Don't know .... ☐ 0

The questionnaire you see before you was published in a book called *Communism, Conformity, and Civil Liberties: A Cross-section of the Nation Speaks Its Mind*, by Samuel A. Stouffer (Doubleday, 1955). As Stouffer explains in his introductory chapter, "More than 6,000 men and women, in all parts of the country and in all walks of life, confided their thoughts . . . . The survey examines in some depth the reactions of Americans to two dangers. One, from the Communist conspiracy outside and inside the country. Two, from those who in thwarting the conspiracy would sacrifice some of the very liberties which the enemy would destroy." Conducted from May through July of 1954, the survey was administered by "over 500 skilled interviewers" from the American Institute of Public Opinion (better known as the Gallup Poll) and the National Opinion Research Center. Its mandate: to answer the question, "Is the American public in a state of pathological fear?"

22. A. Some people say that Americans are getting more distrustful or suspicious of each other than they used to be. Have you thought about this recently, one way or another?

(36)

Yes ———————☐ 1*
No ———————☐ 2
Don't know ———☐ 0

*B. **IF YES:** Have you talked with anybody about this subject, one way or another?

(37)

Yes ———————☐ 1
No ———————☐ 2
Don't know ———☐ 0

23. A. What is your own opinion? Do you think Americans are getting more suspicious of others, or less suspicious?

(38)

More ———————☐ 1*
Same ———————☐ 2
Less ———————☐ 3
Never suspicious ———☐ 4
Don't know ———————☐ 0

*B. **IF MORE:** Why do you say this? In what ways?

29. In some communities, people have been asked to report to the F. B. I. any neighbors or acquaintances who they suspect might be Communists.

A. As far as you know, has this idea been suggested in your city (town, community)?

(46)

Yes ———————☐ 1**
No ———————☐ 2*
Don't know ———☐ 0*

*B. **IF NO OR DON'T KNOW:** Have you read or heard about this idea?

(47)

Yes ———————☐ 1**
No ———————☐ 2
Don't know ———☐ 0

C. **IF YES TO EITHER A OR B: Have you discussed this idea, one way or another, in conversations with anybody?

(48)

Yes ———————☐ 1
No ———————☐ 2
Don't know ———☐ 0

30. A. <u>On the whole,</u> do you think it is a good idea or a bad idea for people to report to the F.B.I. any neighbors or acquaintances whom they suspect of being Communists?

(49)

Good idea ———————☐ 1*
Bad idea ———————☐ 2**
Don't know ———————☐ 0

31. Do you or don't you think the government should have the right to listen in on people's private telephone conversations, in order to get evidence against Communists?

(54)

Yes ———————☐ 1
No ———————☐ 2
Don't know ———————☐ 0

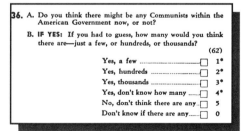

36. A. Do you think there might be any Communists within the American Government now, or not?

B. **IF YES:** If you had to guess, how many would you think there are—just a few, or hundreds, or thousands?

(62)

Yes, a few ———————☐ 1*
Yes, hundreds ———————☐ 2*
Yes, thousands ———————☐ 3*
Yes, don't know how many ———☐ 4*
No, don't think there are any ☐ 5
Don't know if there are any ———☐ 0

42. **A.** Do you think there are any Communists teaching in American public schools, or not?

B. IF YES: If you had to guess, how many would you think— just a few, or hundreds, or thousands?

(73)

Yes, a few .... ☐ 1*

Yes, hundreds .... ☐ 2*

Yes, thousands .... ☐ 3*

Yes, don't know how many ...... ☐ 4*

No, don't think there are any ☐ 5

Don't know if there are any ...... ☐ 0

*C. IF ANY YES ANSWER: How much danger is there that these Communists in public schools can hurt the country— a great danger, some danger, not much danger, or no danger?

(74)

Great .... ☐ 1

Some .... ☐ 2

Not much .... ☐ 3

None .... ☐ 4

Don't know ...... ☐ 0

43. If the school board in your community were to say, some day, that there were no Communists teaching in your schools, would you feel pretty sure it was true, or not?

(75)

Would feel it was true ...... ☐ 1

Would not .... ☐ 2

Don't know .... ☐ 0

The accompanying excerpts from the answers to the questionnaire illustrate how Joe McCarthy, among many others, was able to rise to power so quickly, on so little merit, to such devastating effect.

"It's like a germ. It can spread. Communists are a danger when they talk to ignorant people. Ignorant people can be used by Communists to get more converts. I think ignorant people are most likely to become Communists, but still, I always had a feeling that Mr. and Mrs. Roosevelt may have been Communists."
—housewife, New Jersey

"Communists get children into cellars, educating them in warfare, and training them to go into secret places."
—housewife, Massachusetts

52. **A.** When a man refuses to tell a Congressional committee whether he ever was a Communist, do you think he probably was a Communist, or not?

B. IF PROBABLY WAS: Would you be almost sure he was a Communist, or would you have some doubt?

(13)

Almost sure .... ☐ 6
Have some doubt .... ☐ 7
Probably not .... ☐ 8
Don't know .... ☐ Y

53. **A.** Can you think of any reason why a person would refuse to tell a committee whether he'd ever been a Communist, if he *really never had been?*

(14)

Yes .... ☐ *
No .... ☐ X

*B. IF YES: What sort of reasons might he have for refusing to answer?

54. Sometimes a man says he refuses to answer certain questions about Communism because he does not want to be forced to testify against his former friends. Should he be punished very severely, severely, not too severely, or not at all?

(15)

Very severely .... ☐ 6
Severely .... ☐ 7
Not too severely .... ☐ 8
Not at all .... ☐ 9
Don't know .... ☐ Y

55. It has been said that some loyal Americans won't take Government jobs today for fear of unjust attacks on their reputations. Have you ever heard this, or read of it?

(16)

Yes .... ☐ 6
No .... ☐ 7
Don't know ...... ☐ Y

59. **A.** Suppose you discovered that one of your friends today had been a Communist ten years ago, although you are sure he is not now. Would you break your friendship with him, or not?

(37)

Yes .... ☐ 6
No .... ☐ 7
Don't know ..... ☐ Y

B. Suppose you discovered that one of your good friends today had been a Communist until recently, although he says he is not now. Would you break your friendship with him, or not?

(38)

Yes .... ☐ 6
No .... ☐ 7
Don't know ..... ☐ Y

They are working mostly among Negroes. That Paul Robeson caused a lot of trouble."

—housewife, Oklahoma

Communists have infiltrated into the school system. We know that teachers in Harvard are avowed Communists. They are spreading Communism in every way they can." —housewife, Texas

I have had contacts with Communists for ten years as a labor leader. I know their methods--how a few individuals can take control of seven or eight thousand people." —president, CIO local, New Jersey

Looks like so many foreigners who have settled in this country have been Communists and lowered the morale of people by propaganda." —housewife, Alabama

PAUL ROBESON

At a press conference in Los Angeles recently, Paul Robeson announced his intentions of returning to the concert stage and "his people." The Robeson story has never been fully told. We believe that any American, no matter to what degree the public has pre-judged the case against him, ought to be able to get his story before the public. This is the reason why we are publishing this story and why Carl Rowan was willing to write it. Of course, the reader will have to remain keenly aware of the places in which Robeson is speaking and to make its own judgment as to the merits of Robeson's remarks. Mr. Rowan, author of three books, lecturer and recipient of many prizes in journalism, is a staff writer on the Minneapolis Tribune.

HAS PAUL ROBESON BETRAYED THE NEGRO?

Singer says cowardly Negro leaders failed to back him in struggle for "my people"

Once the leading light to blacks the world over, Paul Robeson parlayed a brilliant stage, film, and recording career into the position he enjoyed throughout the forties--as a political activist who lent his considerable presence to the Progressive Party, the National Negro Congress, the left-leaning unions of the CIO, and the Council on African Affairs. That would have been enough to bring him to the attention of J. Edgar Hoover, but Robeson was also a vocal--and quite unapologetic--Communist sympathizer. For a time, his stature permitted him a certain amount of license, and he was able to flaunt his affinity for the politics of the Soviet Union--as he did by cabling congratulations to Joseph Stalin on his seventieth birthday, and by stating that "Negroes won't fight Russia" in a speech made in Paris at the World Congress of Partisans of Peace in 1949.

But 1949 marked the beginning of the end for Robeson. His notorious Peekskill concert of August 27, organized by a left-wing theatrical agency, provoked one of the ugliest riots in the history of this country. Undaunted, Robeson gave a second concert on September 4, joined by Pete Seeger and other performers of shared political sympathies. Another riot ensued (described with frightening clarity by Howard Fast in his recent memoir, *Being Red*). Now Robeson began to lose the support not only of the black community but even of some of his former champions, like Eleanor Roosevelt. With controversy swirling about him, Robeson had his passport revoked in 1950 by the State Department. Now he was a prisoner in a hostile country--his own.

Invitations to perform grew understandably scarce in the wake of the Peekskill riots, and film or television appearances were out of the question. Cut off from his large international following, Robeson's public activities were reduced to attending parties at the Soviet Embassy in Washington, where he was awarded the International Stalin Peace Prize in 1953 (that must have endeared him to the Feds!), and testifying before HUAC in 1956, where he earned a contempt citation for his belligerence.

By the time *Ebony* magazine published Carl T. Rowan's lengthy interview, "Has Paul Robeson Betrayed the Negro?" (October 1957), Robeson was a broken and embittered man. Although he reminds Rowan that he had testified under oath in 1946 that he was not then and had never been a member of the Communist party, he cannot resist adding, "I just can't help feeling kindly toward a country that has no color prejudice, a country that restrains these Western white boys who want to wipe out all the colored people . . . . Now my believing this does not mean that I'm part of any world conspiracy. It just means that I've decided not to take any more stuff off these crackers. If they want to put me on trial for treason for that, fine."

"IRON CURTAIN LOOK IS HERE"

ON THIS AMERICAN MODEL AND HANGING ALONGSIDE HER IS A COMPLETE AND STYLISH SOVIET WARDROBE. THE TOTAL COST, EXCLUDING HAT, IS $401.40

IRON CURTAIN LOOK IS HERE

U.S. ENVOY'S WIFE FINDS MOSCOW MODES HIGH PRICED, WIDE SHOULDERED, NOT VERY HANDSOME

The slender gams of the girl above give her away as American. The clothes are not. They are new Soviet styles brought home by Mrs. Alan G. Kirk, wife of the recent U.S. ambassador. Here is almost the entire wardrobe for an Iron Curtain look as decreed by Soviet designers. Displayed in Bonwit Teller's, New York, the Moscow modes excited most interest by their cost, translated from rubles: suit $120, dress $128, coat $155, shoes $14.50, bag $19.80, gloves $18.10.

To an American the handsomest garment was the traditional fur hat, which is not considered particularly chic in the U.S.S.R. The rest, drab and stiff, did not do much for the model. They might have done even less had she also worn the other two staples of the wardrobe, an anatomically unique bra, shaped like a double-barrelled shotgun, and knitted bloomers of a shade one observer calls "MVD blue" because it is the color of a Russian secret policeman's cap.

CONTINUED ON NEXT PAGE 119

"**T**he slender gams of the girl above give her away as American." Talk about national chauvinism! Of all the rumors that circulated about the Russians in the fifties, the one about the thick ankles of their womenfolk had to be the most vicious. This article, from a 1952 issue of *Life*, goes on to describe two items of apparel not shown: "an anatomically unique bra, shaped like a double-barrelled shotgun, and knitted bloomers of a shade one observer calls 'MVD blue' because it is the color of a Russian secret policeman's cap." We have no reliable intelligence on the bloomers, but the bra must have been smuggled out of the U.S.S.R. in a diplomatic pouch, because by 1953 every Hollywood starlet from Mamie Van Doren on down appeared to be wearing it.

"IRON CURTAIN GASOLINE COSTS 5 TIMES MORE THAN YOU PAY HERE"

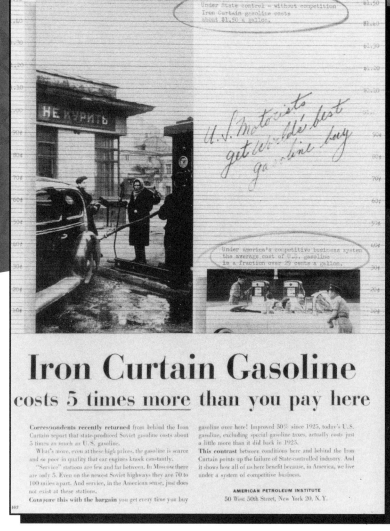

Under State control – without competition Iron Curtain gasoline costs about $1.50 a gallon.

U.S. Motorists get World's best gasoline buy

Under America's competitive business system the average cost of U.S. gasoline is a fraction over 29 cents a gallon.

Iron Curtain Gasoline
costs 5 times more than you pay here

Correspondents recently returned from behind the Iron Curtain report that state-produced Soviet gasoline costs about 5 times as much as U.S. gasoline.

What's more, even at these high prices, the gasoline is scarce and so poor in quality that car engines knock constantly.

"Service" stations are few and far between. In Moscow there are only 5. Even on the newest Soviet highways they are 70 to 100 miles apart. And service, in the American sense, just does not exist at these stations.

Compare this with the bargain you get every time you buy

gasoline over here! Improved 50% since 1925, today's U.S. gasoline, excluding special gasoline taxes, actually costs just a little more than it did back in 1925.

This contrast between conditions here and behind the Iron Curtain points up the failure of State-controlled industry. And it shows how all of us here benefit because, in America, we live under a system of competitive business.

AMERICAN PETROLEUM INSTITUTE
50 West 50th Street, New York 20, N. Y.

Of course, gasoline also cost *five times more* throughout most of Europe in 1955, when the American Petroleum Institute ran this advertisement. But why nitpick? As the copywriter points out, "even at these high prices, the gasoline is scarce and so poor in quality that car engines knock constantly." (Funny, my Ford Pinto had the same problem . . .) He also implies that Soviet service station attendants don't offer to clean your windshields and check the air in your tires. (The scum!) Perhaps if the Soviets hadn't wasted all their time on that Sputnik contraption, they could have built more gas stations. Now: When can we move to that fabled land where the "competitive business system" has kept the cost of gas down to twenty-nine cents a gallon?

Femininity gets short shrift in Russia, where women wield pneumatic drills, not lipsticks.

WOMEN

Russia's second-class citizens

By JULIE WHITNEY Russian-born wife of an American newspaperman

Amazonian statue in Gorki Central Park, Moscow, encourages women to go into athletics

"Long hair--short mind" is a well-known Russian proverb. Russian men of the lower classes still "teach" their wives--in other words, beat them. They, in turn, console themselves with the proverb: "If he doesn't beat me, he doesn't love me."

Russia is basically a patriarchal country. This is so despite the Communist regime's opening most of the traditionally male careers to women and even forcing women into competition with men in many fields. Women dig the ditches, build the roads, lay the bricks, drive the tractors, hoe the

crops and harvest them. If Soviet women went on strike tomorrow, the greater part of Soviet life would come to a halt. But if anyone thinks that heavy manual labor makes the Russian women happy, he is wrong.

True, many Russian women get good educations and become doctors, teachers, engineers, scientists and party workers. A few have become famous like Pasha Angelina, the star tractor driver; Dr. Maria Kovrygina, now Minister of Health; and Yekaterina Furtseva, Communist party careerist,

continued

Written for *Look* in 1954 by the "Russian-born wife of an American newspaperman," Julie Whitney, "Women--Russia's Second-Class Citizens" is a bitter indictment of the sorry lot of the women of the U.S.S.R. "A woman in Russia has a chance to be almost anything," Whitney avers, "except a woman. Even today, in a relatively cosmopolitan Moscow, a good-looking, well-dressed girl wearing make-up is one of three things: a foreigner, an actress or a prostitute. . . . The majority of statues of women in Russian parks wear brassieres and gym pants! Needless to say, there is no 'Miss U.S.S.R.'" Whitney concludes with the damning information that in Moscow, with its population of five million, "there are just two beauty parlors which by Western standards deserve the name. The other half-dozen are 'medical cosmetic institutions.'" I say, let's drop the H-bomb and put them out of their misery.

SOVIET WOMAN 2 1966

Quite a different story is told in the pages of *Soviet Woman* magazine, you can be sure. In the second issue, dated 1966, one finds the inspirational "Soviet Woman--Active and Equal Builder of Communism." Based on an interview with N. V. Podgorny, Chairman of the Presidium of the Supreme Soviet, this article enumerates, with mind-numbing detail, Russia's 860,000 women deputies (43 percent of all Soviet deputies), the 93,000 women elected to the executive committees of the local Soviets, the 2,369 women elected People's Judges in 1965, the 88,000 women awarded the title of Mother Heroine for excellence in the field of family raising, and on and on. And in recognition of these and other contributions to the State, the Presidium of the Supreme Soviet was now declaring March 8 International Women's Day and making it a national holiday.

No "Miss U.S.S.R.," indeed! *Every single one* of Russia's women qualifies for that distinction--though whether Bert Parks would recognize them as such remains open to debate.

As the movie industry had already discovered, the threat of the Red Menace, however much it appeared in the headlines, did not translate automatically into big box-office entertainment. Television, which did not require a paying audience, would make its own attempt to bring the Cold War into the living rooms of America, but in the end it, too, would have to admit defeat.

According to J. Fred MacDonald's seminal study, *Television and the Red Menace: The Video Road to Vietnam*, a number of anti-Communist TV series went on the air during the fifties. The 1951 season offered *Foreign Intrigue*, *Passport to Danger*, and *Dangerous Assignment*. *Biff Baker, U.S.A.* ran on CBS in 1952; it posited an American in the import-export biz who happily does a bit of spying for Uncle Sam as he travels from country to country sewing up deals. Herb Philbrick's pulse-pounding *I Led Three Lives* premiered in 1953, and ran in syndication for three seasons and 117 episodes. *The Man Called X*, *I Spy*, and *Soldiers of Fortune* all did their part to defeat the Communist conspiracy during the 1955 season, and *O.S.S.* (1957), *Behind Closed Doors* (1958), and *Counterthrust* (1960) later registered as Hoover-approved entertainments. But only *Foreign Intrigue* and *I Led Three Lives* lasted longer than a single season, and none of the anti-Commie series garnered ratings to compete with the day's top situation comedies, westerns, and variety shows.

There were, of course, a number of "specials" that addressed, or dramatized, the Red Menace problem throughout the decade. *Nightmare in Red*, a history of Communist Russia, ran on NBC in December of 1955. CBS distinguished itself with "The Day North America Is Attacked," the debut episode of its 1956 *Air Power* series, which was narrated by Walter Cronkite and overseen by the Defense Department. This was an hour-long dramatization-- filmed at defense installations and air bases--that showed exactly how our military would respond if the Russians dispatched 1,100 aircraft to attack us from all directions.

Photofest

Produced without the help of the Defense Department, *Darkness at Noon*, a dramatization of Arthur Koestler's anti-totalitarian novel, was broadcast by NBC on May 2, 1955. As a play, it had been hailed as "brilliant anti-Communist propaganda" (*Herald Tribune*) when it opened on Broadway in January 1951, and ultimately won the Drama Critics Circle Award as the year's best play. The NBC production offered a less stellar cast than the original, but was still well received. (Oddly enough, Arthur Miller's 1953 drama, *The Crucible*, an allegory of the McCarthy witch-hunts, did not make it to television during the fifties. Probably just an oversight.)

More entertaining still were the frequent TV appearances of Senator Joseph McCarthy. Already a veteran of many radio interviews during the late forties, by 1950 McCarthy was a frequent commentator on shows like *Meet the Press* and *Chronoscope*. On one *Meet the Press* appearance early in 1950, McCarthy was asked what his reasons were for so energetically chasing Communists. "It's just one of those tasks that someone has to do," the self-sacrificing saint replied. He did yeoman duty for the Republican cause just before the 1952 Presidential election, when he accused Democratic candidate Adlai Stevenson on TV of being a Commie stooge and an old crony of Alger Hiss--"the arch-traitor of our times"--to boot. So much for Adlai's campaign.

But by 1954, McCarthy's shield of invulnerability was starting to crack. On March 9, Edward R. Murrow's *See It Now* offered revealing videotape of America's favorite bully being his usual nasty self interrogating witnesses before his Senate subcommittee. McCarthy demanded equal time, and got it, on an April 6 broadcast of *See It Now*. It wasn't enough. Damage had been done, and the live television broadcast of what came to be known as the Army-McCarthy hearings was the coup de grâce. The 187 hours of television time given those hearings exposed McCarthy once and for all as the biggest lout in the land. His colleagues in the Senate must have concurred, as they voted 67-22 to censure McCarthy in 1954. Two years later, the whiskey-soaked demagogue died in disgrace. What television giveth, television taketh away.

But television's last word on the Soviet threat was submitted in 1959, when the cartoon series *Rocky and His Friends* debuted. After watching the bungling of Red agents Boris Badenov and Natasha Fatále, America's children would never again cower in quite the same way when the epithet "Communist" was uttered.

JOE STALIN: WIFE KILLER!

De-Stalinization took many forms. Not to kick a guy when he's dead and buried, but Stalin endured a number of indignities at the hands of Khrushchev's crack propaganda team. One of the smarmiest was reported in the August 1956 issue of *He* magazine, a beacon of editorial integrity during the Pinko-infested fifties. "Joe Stalin: Wife Killer!" manages to blend *Pravda* and *The Police Gazette* into a seamless whole. It's a sordid tale of a fatal dispute between Stalin and his wife over his rural collectivization program in 1932. All the classic elements of domestic tragedy are here: a jilted lover (Lenin, no less!), a crime committed in the heat of Party deviationism, and a coverup that held for over twenty years. Incredibly, "Joe Stalin: Wife Killer!" failed to be nominated for a Pulitzer for Investigative Reporting.

RARE PHOTO OF STALIN'S WIFE'S BODY AFTER MURDER.

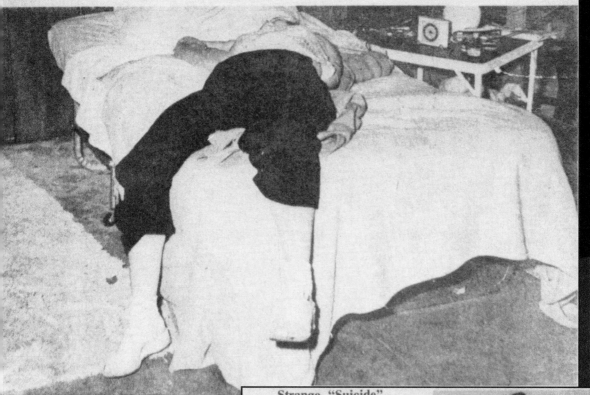

Strange "Suicide"

In view of this, it is all the more strange that she engaged Stalin in the semi-public argument which led to her death. It was an evening in November of 1932. Stalin and his wife attended a party at the palatial home of Marshal Klimente Voroshilov, currently Soviet head of state.

There were many upper echelon Red leaders present. The conversation was about Stalin's program for the collectivization of agriculture which had brought on famine and roused the peasant population to mass protests. Mme. Alliluyeva debated with her husband the wisdom of his policies in this matter. Stalin grew purple with anger and rebuked her viciously. She left the party and he followed shortly afterwards. A

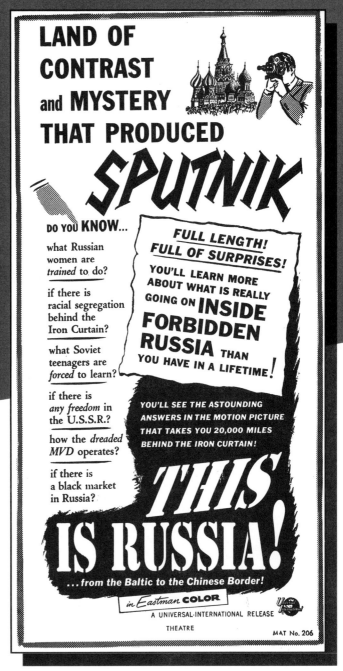

LAND OF CONTRAST and MYSTERY THAT PRODUCED **SPUTNIK**

DO YOU KNOW...

what Russian women are *trained to do?*

if there is racial segregation behind the Iron Curtain?

what Soviet teenagers are *forced* to learn?

if there is *any freedom* in the U.S.S.R.?

how the *dreaded MVD* operates?

if there is a black market in Russia?

FULL LENGTH! FULL OF SURPRISES!

YOU'LL LEARN MORE ABOUT WHAT IS REALLY GOING ON **INSIDE FORBIDDEN RUSSIA** THAN YOU HAVE IN A LIFETIME!

YOU'LL SEE THE ASTOUNDING ANSWERS IN THE MOTION PICTURE THAT TAKES YOU 20,000 MILES BEHIND THE IRON CURTAIN!

THIS IS RUSSIA!

...*from the Baltic to the Chinese Border!*

in *Eastman* COLOR

A UNIVERSAL-INTERNATIONAL RELEASE

THEATRE

MAT No. 206

Hollywood was at a loss after Stalin's death in 1953. His awesome specter had informed the politics of so many films--and suddenly he was gone, replaced by second-stringers like Georgi Malenkov (who had to resign in disgrace as Premier less than two years later because his agricultural program had been dumb), and Marshal Bulganin (the new Premier who was so anonymous that most Americans assumed he was just a guest star on *Gunsmoke*). Party First Secretary Nikita Khrushchev seemed to be the real power, but he still looked like the hayseed he once was--and, after all, he *was* just a secretary.

NFM-C 134

Photofest

BREAKS THROUGH THE FORBIDDEN BARRIER!

No man can pay the price for what this woman offers!

Love that knows no boundaries... passion that explodes a cold war into a jet-hot battle of the sexes!

HOWARD HUGHES'
JET PILOT

Starring

JOHN WAYNE · JANET LEIGH
AND THE
U.S. AIR FORCE

with JAY C. FLIPPEN · PAUL FIX · HANS CONRIED

TECHNICOLOR®

RKO RADIO PICTURE

Released by
UNIVERSAL-
INTERNATIONAL®

Directed by JOSEF von STERNBERG · Written and Produced by JULES FURTHMAN

Small wonder, then, that the films made in the second half of the decade contained only a residue of the dread that had permeated the earlier Cold War movies. In fact, Hollywood after 1955 was barely able to rouse itself to peevishness when it came to the Russians. In 1956, audiences were treated to the odd spectacle of Katherine Hepburn as a Soviet officer opposite Bob Hope in *The Iron Petticoat*, and George Orwell's 1948 novel *1984* was finally adapted for the big screen. Cyd Charisse reprised the Garbo role in *Silk Stockings*, the 1957 remake of *Ninotchka*, with singing and dancing added at no extra charge. A bit of nostalgia for Uncle Joe was detectable in *The Girl in the Kremlin*, which posed the question, "Is Stalin Alive?" while showing a curious world what Zsa Zsa Gabor would look like with her head shaved. But the highlight of 1957 was the long-delayed *Jet Pilot*, which RKO studio head Howard Hughes had been fiddling with since 1950, when it was originally scheduled for release. As "the most delectable member of the military ever to come out from behind the Iron Curtain," Janet Leigh plays a curvaceous Soviet captain who bamboozles Air Force Colonel John Wayne into stealing a jet plane for her bosses to study. Inevitably, though, she falls for the Duke, and the Central Committee has to go back to the drawing board.

Ultimately, it was left to such B-film fantasies as *Invaders from Mars* (1953), *Invasion of the Body Snatchers* (1956), and *I Married a Monster from Outer Space* (1958) to express allegorically the fear of infection and takeover by alien (read: Red) forces that many Americans were clinging to. Today, those films feel much more sincere than the forced goodwill of *Jet Pilot* and its ilk.

ICBM

The Inter-Continental Ballistic Missile: the proposed "ultimate weapon." The ne plus ultra of long-range bombardment missiles, the ICBM was designed to do what air-to-air and ship-to-shore missiles could not: deliver an H-bomb warhead to a target thousands of miles away. But who would develop it first? This article by Hanson Baldwin, military editor for *The New York Times*, which appeared in the March 16, 1956, issue of *Collier's* magazine, outlined the stakes in the race America had to win:

"This giant ocean-spanning, mountain-leaping rocket--mated to a hydrogen warhead with a destructive capability of megatons (millions of tons of TNT)--is a supreme instrument of offense. It arches so high (600 to 800 miles above the earth), and moves so fast (12,000 to 16,000 miles an hour) that, once it has been launched, defense against it will be nearly, if not entirely, impossible. The German V-2, the small 200-mile-range forerunner of the ICBM, bombarded London during World War II, and even the conventional explosives then used in the warhead caused thousands of casualties and blew whole buildings apart. The ICBM will--when developed--threaten every city on earth, not merely with damage but with destruction.

"The implications are frightening--and sobering. In the early period of the coming ICBM era, before radar missile-detection and possible antimissile defenses are developed, an enemy could probably devastate the United States with a surprise ballistic missile bombardment before we could even detect the attack--much less before we could launch a retaliatory attack. One or two missiles for each of our 50 biggest cities might cause 10,000,000 to 50,000,000 casualties, knock out perhaps a third of our industrial capacity, and turn parts of America into radioactive deserts.

How is the race going?

No one--in Washington or Moscow--can answer that positively. 'We just don't know,' a high U.S. official says.

But many of our Intelligence officials and some of our scientists believe Russia leads today."

SPUTNIK

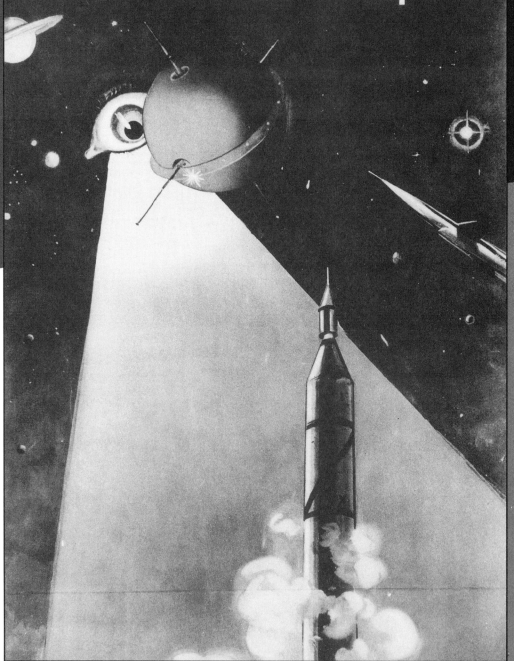

THE ENEMY THAT WATCHES...
behind the veil of Space!

"SOVIET FIRES EARTH SATELLITE INTO SPACE; IT IS CIRCLING THE GLOBE AT 18,000 M.P.H.; SPHERE TRACKED IN 4 CROSSINGS OVER U.S."

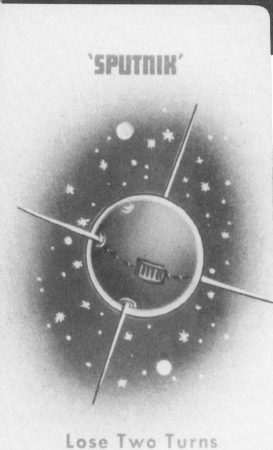

That banner headline from *The New York Times* of October 5, 1957, sent chills down America's spine. Although Ike tried to downplay the significance of the Sputnik launch, he quickly learned that to most of his countrymen the news carried the same implications as the arrival of Armageddon. Not that the Sputnik satellite was itself so formidable; at 184 pounds and with a diameter of twenty-two inches, it couldn't have dropped anything bigger than an apple on us. But what it symbolized was like a million tons of TNT: The Russkies now controlled the heavens above. (And those godless Reds didn't even *believe* in heaven!)

Total panic

didn't set in, though, for another two months. It was then, on the sixteenth anniversary of Pearl Harbor, that newspapers around the country reported a disaster of unspeakable proportions: the Vanguard rocket carrying our answer to Sputnik--a puny four-pound satellite about the size of a softball--had exploded after rising just two feet off its launching pad at Cape Canaveral. (Two feet! The Russians orbit the globe four times, and we get *two feet* into space!) The shock--and the humiliation--could only have been greater had the Commies set up a slave labor camp on Main Street in Muncie, Indiana.

Having apparently lost the Space Race at the starting gate, America went on Red Alert. Bomb drills became more familiar to schoolchildren than recess, and owners of bomb shelters--considered quacks by their neighbors just a few months earlier--were suddenly the most popular folks on the block. Films like *Spy in the Sky* appeared at drive-ins, and even children's toys like the Satellite Space Race Card Game reflected our national obsession.

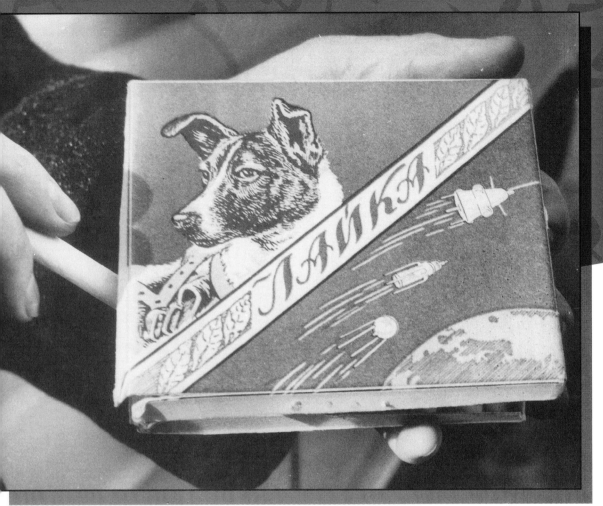

   Then on January 31, 1958, we recovered a small measure of our self-respect. It was on that night that the Army finally made a successful launch that put a satellite into orbit. So what if the Soviets in the meantime had put three satellites into orbit, including one that carried the dog that won Russia's heart, the brave little mutt Laika? (Her commemorative cigarette pack is shown here; unfortunately, she didn't live to enjoy it.) At least we were on the scoreboard. Now the Space Race was truly a race once more. And with God on our side . . .

(A final thought about all those bomb drills that taught us how to curl into a ball at a moment's notice: How exactly was that skill supposed to save us from an atomic blast that could level an entire city on impact? Just curious.)

CIVIL DEFENSE

Archive Photos

FALLOUT SHELTER

FALLOUT
SHELTER

ACCEPTED BY THE OFFICE OF CIVIL DEFENSE AND
MOBILIZATION AS PROVIDING ALMOST ABSOLUTE
PROTECTION AGAINST FALLOUT RADIATION

FIBERGLASS   CONSTRUCTION
PLUS 9" OF CONCRETE
ACCOMODATES 6 PEOPLE

$2395 INSTALLED

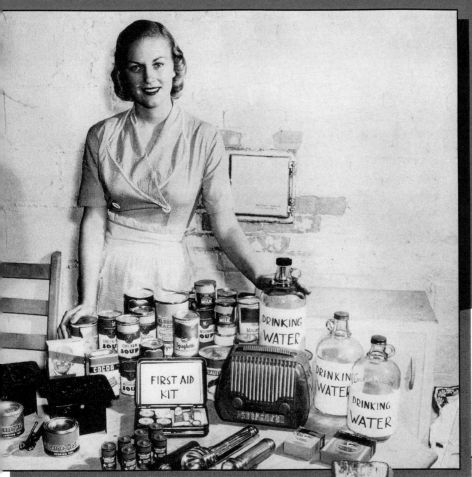

Okay, now you're in your shelter. You've got your bottled drinking water. You've got your Canned Heat. You've got Campbell's soups, cocoa, coffee, and condensed milk. You've got flashlights and plenty of batteries. You've got a can opener. You've got a radio. You've got a shovel and a bucket of sand. Now all you need is for the Russkies to drop the Big One. So where the heck *is* it, already?

Archive Photos

If Stalin ruled through fear and intimidation, Khrushchev's considerable success had to be attributed more to guile and an infallible sense of showmanship. Not that Nikita couldn't be ruthless when the situation demanded; his response to the Hungarian uprising in November of 1956 was Stalinesque in its brutality, and of course there were those accounts of the 400,000 lives he had snuffed out over a two-year period while overseeing the Ukraine before the war.

But once he consolidated his power, in 1957, by ousting Molotov, Malenkov, and Kaganovich--old Stalinites all--Khrushchev took and held center stage with an ease that Ike and Nixon were obviously unprepared for. The Sputnik triumph a few months later taught America the valuable lesson that Nikita, he of the gap-toothed grin and the mine-mechanic body, was not to be underestimated. The announcement on March 27, 1958, that Khrushchev had replaced Bulganin as Premier of the Soviet Union, while remaining First Secretary of the Communist Party, was a near-anticlimax. But what Khrushchev had accomplished in five years while rising through the collective leadership to seize control was a more impressive display of political savvy than even Uncle Joe himself had ever exhibited.

The most instructive example of Khrushchev's genius came in 1959, when he trumped his September visit to the U.S.--the first Soviet chief of state ever to arrive on these shores--by seeing to it that a Russian rocket had hit the moon the day before. Nixon tried to downplay the impact of that news by announcing, typically through sources he could not reveal (national security, no doubt), that the Russians had missed the moon on three earlier tries. "It's nothing to get excited about," Nixon reassured *The New York Times*. "Scientifically and educationally we are way ahead of the Soviets." In the meantime, a large sphere bearing metal pennants decorated with the hammer and sickle was resting on the moon, near the Sea of Tranquility. Although our government rejected those Commie flags as proof of ownership, Khrushchev's earlier remarks about Russia's inevitable triumph in the world economy--the infamous "We will bury you!" boast that had so rankled Nixon--now began to take on other implications.

Through the course of his U.S. visit, Khrushchev beamed. He gobbled hot dogs in Des Moines, and charmed the initially hostile American crowds from Pittsburgh to Los Angeles to San Francisco. It was a performance that seemed to mark the beginning of the end of the Cold War. But on May 5, 1960, one of our U-2 "weather observation" planes was reported shot down over Sverdlovsk, an industrial city some 1,300 miles inside Russia's borders. Nikita the Jolly was quickly replaced by his evil twin, Nikita the Rocket-rattling Table-thumper, and the hostilities resumed, as if Des Moines had been only a dream.

By 1962, when Columbia Pictures released the low-budget documentary *"We'll Bury You!,"* Khrushchev had taken on the aspect of King Kong, a monster who "brought half the world to its knees!" (And with that came top billing--over hated rival Mao--as "World Enemy #1!") But his failure of nerve during the Cuban Missile Crisis, late in 1962, hastened the Politburo's perception that the Old Man was slipping, and he was deposed in 1964. His replacement: the vastly uncharismatic Leonid Brezhnev. Communism would never be as much fun again.

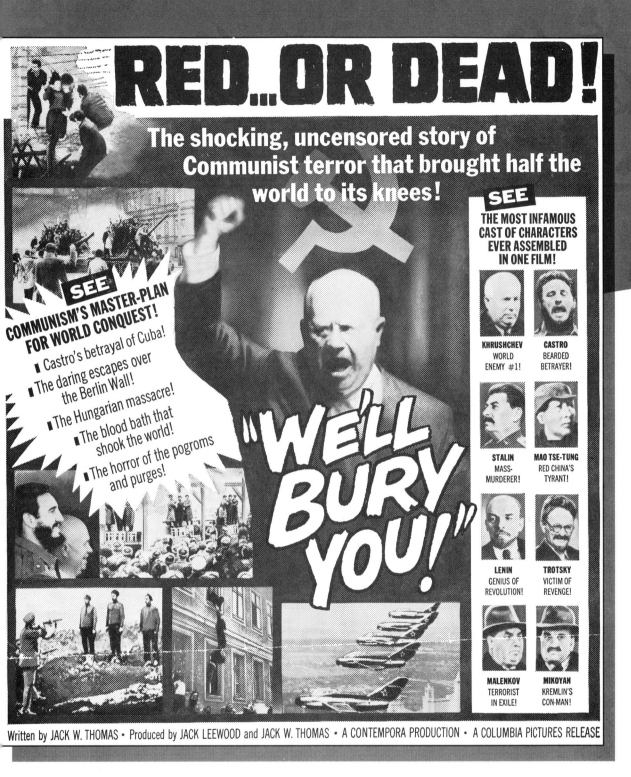

"THIS GODLESS COMMUNISM"

OFFICE OF THE DIRECTOR

UNITED STATES DEPARTMENT OF JUSTICE
FEDERAL BUREAU OF INVESTIGATION

WASHINGTON 25, D. C.

March 13, 1961

I would like to take this opportunity to extend greetings to the readers of Treasure Chest.

Your editor has informed me that this magazine is undertaking a series of stories on communism, and I am pleased to present my views on the importance of understanding this subject. Communism represents the most serious threat facing our way of life. The responsibility of protecting and preserving the freedoms we cherish will soon belong to the members of your generation. The most effective way for you to fight communism is to learn all you can about it. Do this by pursuing the appropriate courses of study at your school and by reading books and other material on this subject. Thus equipped, you will know and understand the nature of communism. This knowledge is most essential, for it helps us recognize and detect the communists as they attempt to infiltrate the various segments of our society.

John Edgar Hoover
Director

TREASURE CHEST of FUN and FACT, Vol. 17, No. 2. Published every two weeks during the school year since March 7, 1946 by GEO. A. PFLAUM, PUBLISHER, INC., 38 WEST FIFTH STREET, DAYTON 2, OHIO. Second-class postage paid at Dayton, Ohio and at additional mailing offices. Single subscription $2.00 per year, in U. S. and $2.40 in Canada and foreign countries. Subscription rates on quantity orders supplied upon request. Printed in U.S.A. Richard J. Voelkel, editor; Barbara A. Snider, associate editor; Victor Keuping, art director; Carl Beacham, copy editor. © 1961 by Geo. A. Pflaum, Publisher, Incorporated. Also publisher of the YOUNG CATHOLIC MESSENGER, JUNIOR CATHOLIC MESSENGER, and OUR LITTLE MESSENGER. James J. Pflaum, editor in chief.

It's not every comic book series that was favored with J. Edgar Hoover's own Good-Commies-Are-Dead-Commies seal of approval, but "This Godless Communism," which ran in ten installments in *Treasure Chest of Fun and Fact* comics in 1961 and 1962, truly earned it. Lovingly illustrated by Reed Crandall, "This Godless Communism" blended fact ("Khrushchev was born 68 years ago in Kalinovka, near Ukrainia") with docudrama (how Stalin rose to power; how Khrushchev implemented de-Stalinization) and scenes of feverish fantasy too numerous to list (a personal favorite: a Red soldier pressing a detonator that blows up the Washington Monument).

Published by the folks who also brought out *Young Catholic Messenger* magazine, "This Godless Communism" understandably was well-seasoned with religious fervor. It's all here: forced labor camps, firing squads, the Hungarian revolt of 1956, the space race, brainwashing, and endless images of octopi and dragons encircling the globe. Not for those who like to recall Khrushchev as a happy-go-lucky chap with a puckish sense of humor.

THIS GODLESS COMMUNISM

WE HAVE SEEN IN THIS SERIES OF STORIES THE WAY IN WHICH RUSSIA'S LEADERS HAVE FOLLOWED THE TEACHINGS OF MARX AND LENIN. BEHIND THEM, THEY HAVE LEFT A BLOODY TRAIL.

THEIR METHODS ARE VERY CHANGEABLE. TO THOSE WHO WILL LISTEN TO TALK OF PEACE, THEY WILL TALK OF PEACE. TO THOSE WHO WILL FALTER BEFORE THREATS OF WAR, THEY WILL THREATEN WAR. BUT BEHIND ALL THIS TALK IS ONE GOAL: WORLD DOMINATION BY ANY MEANS.

CULTURE

TREATY

R. CRANDALL

IN ITS WAKE, COMMUNISM HAS LEFT A TRAIL OF MURDERS, LIES, AND MISERY OF A KIND NEVER BEFORE SEEN IN THE HISTORY OF THE WORLD. IT IS TRULY THE WORK OF THE DEVIL.

ess adroitly illustrated than "This Godless Communism," their contemporary, *Double Talk . . .* and *Two Faces of Communism* still have much to offer to aficionados of virulent Red-baiting. Published as giveaways in 1961 by Dr. Fred C. Schwarz's Christian Anti-Communism Crusade of Houston, these two comic books do not so much tell a story as limn the dangers of Communism in a series of vignettes simple enough for a first-grader to absorb. Invoking CIA Director Allen Dulles's 1960 plea for more education about the threat of international Communism, *Double Talk . . .* and *Two Faces of Communism* present Khrushchev's satanic side to make their point, although the hapless (and anonymous) cartoonist makes him look more like *Candid Camera*'s Allen Funt than Mephistopheles.

"IT'S HAPPENING AS YOU READ THIS!"

So the ads for M-G-M's 1962 film *Escape from East Berlin* proclaimed. Filmed on location "under the very noses of the Communists across the wall," and inspired by the actual January 25, 1962, escape of twenty-eight East Germans via a tunnel under the Wall, *Escape from East Berlin* enjoyed an incredible stroke of luck when, just before its release, another group of East Germans successfully tunneled to the West. The film's advertising material was able to make the most of *The New York Times* headline that appeared on September 19th announcing: "29 E. BERLINERS FLEE THROUGH 400-FOOT TUNNEL." But real genius was evinced by M-G-M's promotion department, which suggested to exhibitors, "From the local junk yard, get some old barbed wire and make a barbed wire and brick wall display for your theatre lobby. It will create talk and interest in the film." No doubt.

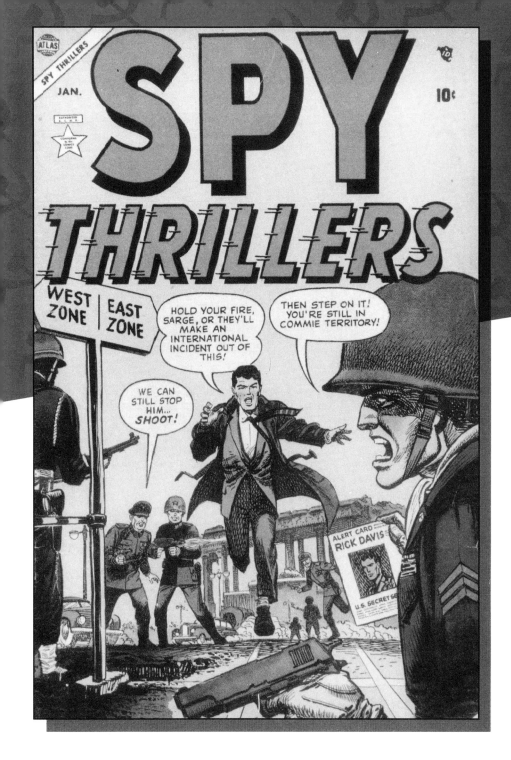

The accompanying cover from the January 1955 issue of *Spy Thrillers* illustrates just how simple life in the divided Germany was before the Wall went up in August of 1961--one mad dash past a couple of guards and you were free! No wonder Stalin once remarked, "Communism in Germany is like putting a saddle on a cow."

FIDEL

Archive Photos

Archive Photos

"BATISTA AND REGIME FLEE CUBA; CASTRO MOVING TO TAKE POWER; MOBS RIOT AND LOOT IN HAVANA."

So read the headline in *The New York Times* of January 2, 1959. The *Times* reported that Batista complained from his new home in the Dominican Republic that Castro's rebels had not only possessed superiority in arms in defeating Batista's army, but also had used guerrilla tactics "simliar to those of the Chinese Communists." No fair! No fair! (But then, *any* of us would feel cranky the next day if our casinos and parking meters had been trashed and looted by our loving constituents.) Batista's eldest son, Ruben, checked in from his new digs in Jacksonville, Florida, to predict trouble for Cuba because some of the rebels were "militant Communists and fellow-travelers." (Meaning, they wouldn't know how to run a casino properly?)

Señor Castro, as the *Times* referred to him, was that rarity--a genuinely charismatic Communist leader. He also was something of a loose cannon; Khrushchev quickly learned he couldn't control him. And in the 1961 Bay of Pigs fiasco, President Kennedy and the CIA learned that Castro's popularity with Cuba's populace was not to be underestimated.

Leaving aside those hilarious tales of the CIA's attempts to assassinate Fidel--the poisoned cigar and the exploding seashell (or was it the exploding cigar and the poisoned seashell?)--we now move ahead to October of 1962.

RED STAR OVER CUBA

THE RUSSIAN ASSAULT ON THE WESTERN HEMISPHERE

NATHANIEL WEYL

This is the shocking story of how a People's Republic was born within 90 miles of our United States frontiers. It is the equally shocking story of the part played by our own State Department in handing Cuba over to the bearded dictator Fidel Castro, despite specific warnings from two recent Cuban Ambassadors that Castro's movement was a Communist one, Soviet inspired.

"As early as 1949," says Weyl, "Fidel Castro was not merely an implacable enemy of the United States, but a trusted Soveit agent as well."

Reading like a detective story, *Red Star Over Cuba* documents his charges, concluding that "we were hood-winked about Cuba by naive sentimentalists, deluded liberals and philocommunists."

With American missiles already installed in Turkey, Italy, and England, Khrushchev needed to show the U.S. that he could not be cowed. His answer was the deployment of SS-4 and SS-5 missiles to Cuba, along with light bombers and 40,000 Soviet troops. And there they sat, ninety miles from Florida. Khrushchev later would say that the missiles were sent to protect Cuba from the big bully to the north, but it was really his last-ditch effort to balance the scales of power, which had been tipping to the advantage of the U.S. ever since the triumph of Sputnik. But Kennedy stared down Khrushchev, and the missiles and troops were stamped RETURN TO SENDER.

With his days in power numbered, Khrushchev nonetheless invited Castro to the U.S.S.R., not once but twice. The first visit took place in 1963, when Castro flew to Moscow in secrecy to attend the May Day celebration, at which he shared the place of honor above Lenin's tomb with Nikita and the fellows from the Presidium. (Castro's thoughts as the missile-floats rumbled past were not shared--but, hey, they had to do *something* with the damn things after shipping them halfway around the world and back!) In honor of Castro's presence, many of the marchers wore sombreros.

Archive Photos

Later, in January of 1964, Castro visited Khrushchev at his woodsy dacha, where the two leaders strolled through the snow and talked about the good old days. It was to be their last get-together. But even without Nikita to help position his country on the brink of nuclear war, Castro somehow muddled on.

Master of the Red Jab

Ho Chi Minh is waging the kind of war that he knows best. An inside report on America's enemy, North Vietnam.

By BERNARD B. FALL

North Vietnamese army, 400,000 strong, is rated one of the world's best infantry forces.

Ho (at left), still spry at 72, was a leading Communist long before Nikita Khrushchev.

It wasn't classified information, and it wasn't hidden on microfilm inside a pumpkin for ten years. But somehow Bernard Fall's 1962 interview with Ho Chi Minh, then seventy-two, and his prime minister, Pham Van Dong, escaped the notice of the entire population of the Pentagon, despite its publication in one of the country's largest-circulation magazines, *The Saturday Evening Post*. One would at least like to think that our military was unaware of the information in "Master of the Red Jab"; else, how to explain their total unreadiness for precisely the reception in Southeast Asia that Fall prophesies?

And finally, beyond the party, there is the fearsome Vietnam People's Army. The French--who have good reasons to know it well--estimate it to be one of the best combat-infantry forces in the world today . . . . From a 24-man platoon in 1944, the army has grown into a force of 400,000 men, lavishly armed with Soviet automatic weapons. Yet in spite of this modern armament, the army had lost none of its incredible agility in cross-country maneuvering. Whatever training I could see in North Vietnam--none of it was shown to me deliberately--seemed to confirm that the North Vietnamese were as ready as ever to fight in the swamps and jungles of their country. I saw infantrymen dogtrotting along the roads with full field kits in the blazing tropical sun. I saw officers instructing militiamen--there are an estimated 2,000,000 of them--in how to attack concrete bunkers. They were not training to fight against an imaginary enemy but against South Vietnamese--and Americans . . . .

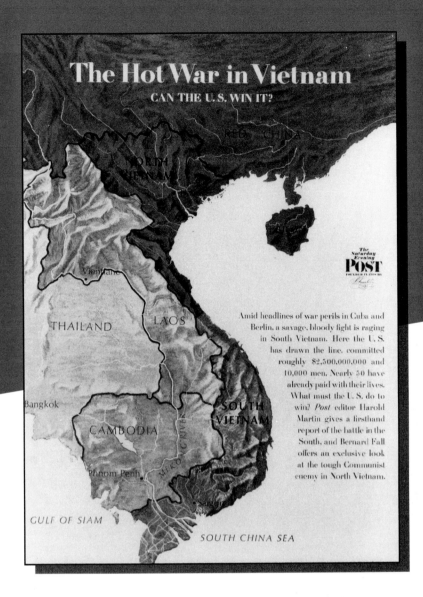

The Hot War in Vietnam
CAN THE U.S. WIN IT?

Amid headlines of war perils in Cuba and Berlin, a savage, bloody fight is raging in South Vietnam. Here the U.S. has drawn the line, committed roughly $2,500,000,000 and 10,000 men. Nearly 50 have already paid with their lives. What must the U.S. do to win? *Post* editor Harold Martin gives a firsthand report of the battle in the South, and Bernard Fall offers an exclusive look at the tough Communist enemy in North Vietnam.

For Americans, this war means not only an economic drain but a political drain. "Americans do not like long, inconclusive wars--and this is going to be a long, inconclusive war," remarked Premier Pham Van Dong. "Thus we are sure to win in the end."

Fall's rueful comment about the readiness of the North Vietnamese--"There is, I fear, some justification for the Communist leader's optimism"--could have served as the epitaph for the American war effort over the next ten years. But the war in Vietnam also accomplished something else: Russia would never again hog center stage as our primary, primal concern. The Cold War would linger on, of course, heating up periodically as world events added fresh fuel. But Vietnam overshadowed even the 1964 "retirement" of Khrushchev, the last epic foe the U.S.S.R. could provide us.

After our mortification in Vietnam mercifully ended, America had to look elsewhere for an enemy worthy of our national hatred. We searched within, and we searched without. And we found what we found. But, quite clearly, it would never be the same as it was during those gloriously satisfying years of fear when Russia haunted each day and every dream.

Soviet Union, 191

*DECLARING DEATH OF S
AND 2 REPUBLICS FOR*

Death Sentence in N

GORBACHEV, LAST SOVIET
U.S. RECOGNIZES REPU
Soviet Union to offi

1991 Gorbachev Has No Role, Gets Set to Resign

VIET UNION, RUSSIA NEW COMMONWEALTH

SCOW

LEADER, RESIGNS; BLICS' INDEPENDENCE

Communist Flag Is Removed; Yeltsin Gets Nuclear Controls

ally die Jan. 1

They lost.

988: Pagan Russia converts to Christianity.

1240: Mongols invade Russia.

1480: Mongol reign ends.

1547: Ivan the Terrible crowned Tsar at age seventeen.

1565: Ivan creates the first secret police.

1682: Peter the Great crowned Tsar.

1762: Catherine the Great seizes the throne.

1812: Napoleon invades and is defeated.

1848: Karl Marx and Friedrich Engels publish *The Communist Manifesto*, which urged workers o
the world to unite in overthrowing capitalism.

1861: Serfs emancipated.

1898: Russian Social Democratic Labor Party, a Marxist group, is formed illegally.

1903: Vladimir I. Lenin leads split from RSDLP and founds Bolshevik Party.

1914: Germany declares war on Russia.

1917: Bolshevik Revolution begins in October (using Russian calendar).

1918: Tsar Nicholas II and family are executed in July.

1919: Comintern is founded with the aim of coordinating the world's Communist parties unde
Soviet control.

1920: Lenin's Red Army defeats the White armies.

1924: Lenin dies; Stalin takes power.

1929: Stalin launches a five-year-plan for forced industrialization and orders collectivization of farms; famine kills as many as fifteen million.

1936: Stalin launches the Great Purge; an estimated twelve to twenty million people are imprisoned or killed for political reasons.

1939: Soviet Union signs non-aggression pact with Nazi Germany.

1941: Germany invades, and is defeated in 1945.

1953: Stalin dies on March 5, an event celebrated in the U.S. by the songs "Stalin Kicked the Bucket" by Ray Anderson, and "The Death of Joe Stalin (Good Riddance)" by Buddy Hawk.

1954: Nikita Khrushchev emerges as ruler of the Soviet Union and launches a political "thaw," freeing millions of prisoners.

1956: Khrushchev publicly acknowledges Stalin-era crimes; he also sends the Soviet army to crush Hungarian revolution.

1961: East Germany erects the Berlin Wall.

1964: Khrushchev is replaced by Leonid Brezhnev, who formulates a doctrine preventing member nations from leaving the Soviet bloc.

1968: Soviets invade Czechoslovakia, crushing the Prague Spring.

1979: Soviet invasion of Afghanistan.

1982: Brezhnev dies after long illness; successor Yuri Andropov dies the following year, and is succeeded by Konstantin Chernenko.

1985: Chernenko dies; he is succeeded by Mikhail Gorbachev, who launches *perestroika* (restructuring) and *glasnost* (openness) programs.

1986: Chernobyl nuclear-reactor accident; Sox blow World Series.

1989: Berlin Wall falls.

1990: McDonald's opens in Moscow in January, signaling America's victory in the Cold War.

Bibliography

Andrews, Bert. *Washington Witch Hunt*. New York: Random House, 1948.

Belfrage, Cedric. *The American Inquisition*, 1945-1960. Indianapolis: Bobbs-Merrill, 19

Calomiris, Angela. *Red Masquerade: Undercover for the F.B.I.* Philadelphia: J. B. Lippincott, 1950.

Conquest, Robert. *Stalin: Breaker of Nations*. New York: Viking, 1991.

Duberman, Martin Bauml. *Paul Robeson*. New York: Alfred A. Knopf, 1988.

Fast, Howard. *Being Red*. Boston: Houghton Mifflin, 1990.

Friedrich, Otto. *City of Nets: A Portrait of Hollywood in the 1940's*. New York: Harper & Row, 1986.

Gentry, Curt. *J. Edgar Hoover: The Man and the Secrets*. New York: W. W. Norton, 1991.

Goldman, Eric F. *The Crucial Decade--and After: America, 1945-1960*. New York: Vintage Books, 1960.

Goodman, Walter. *The Committee*. Baltimore, Maryland: Penguin Books, 1969.

Hyland, William G. *The Cold War Is Over*. New York: Times Books, 1990.

MacDonald, J. Fred. *Television and the Red Menace: The Video Road to Vietnam*. New York: Praeger, 1985.

Mitgang, Herbert. *Dangerous Dossiers*. New York: Ballantine, 1989.

Navasky, Victor S. *Naming Names*. New York: Penguin Books, 1991.

Philbrick, Herbert A. *I Led Three Lives: Citizen, "Communist," Counterspy*. New York: McGraw-Hill, 1952.

Savage, William W., Jr. *Comic Books and America, 1945-1954*. Norman, Oklahoma: University of Oklahoma Press, 1990.

Sayre, Nora. *Running Time: Films of the Cold War*. New York: The Dial Press, 1979.

Seton-Watson, Hugh. *From Lenin to Malenkov: The History of World Communism*. New York: Frederick A. Praeger, 1953.

Sperber, A.M. *Murrow: His Life and Times*. New York: Bantam, 1987.

Stouffer, Samuel A. *Communism, Conformity, and Civil Liberties: A Cross-section of the Nation Speaks Its Mind*. Garden City, New York: Doubleday, 1955.

Copyright Acknowledgments

About the Author

MICHAEL BARSON is the editor of the popular postcard books *Lost, Lonely & Vicious*, *Born to Be Bad*, and *Boy Loves Girl, Girl Loves Boy*. He also edited *Flywheel, Shyster, and Flywheel: The Marx Brothers' Lost Radio Show*, which has been translated into six languages and dramatized by the BBC. His work has appeared in *The New York Times*, *Entertainment Weekly*, *Rolling Stone*, *American Film*, *Newsday*, *Publishers Weekly*, and *Nostalgia*, and he been a frequent guest on NPR's "Fresh Air" program. Barson has an M.A. in Popular Culture and a Ph.D. in American Culture from Bowling Green State University in Ohio, where he taught for five years. He lives in New Jersey with his wife, Jean, and their sons, Benjamin and Daniel.